# Lightweight Alpine Climbing with Peter Croft

**Peter Croft and Steve Boga**

## STACKPOLE BOOKS

Published by
STACKPOLE BOOKS
5067 Ritter Road
Mechanicsburg, PA 17055

Printed in the United States of America

10 9 8 7 6 5 4 3 2 1

First Edition

Cover photo by Chris Falkenstein: Peter Croft nears the summit of the north ridge of Mount Conness, Yosemite National Park
Cover design by Kathleen D. Peters
Illustrations by Thomas Aubrey

**Library of Congress Cataloging-in-Publication Data**

Croft, Peter, 1958–
    Lightweight alpine climbing with Peter Croft / Peter Croft and Steve Boga. — 1st ed.
        p.   cm.
    ISBN 0-8117-2841-2
    1. Mountaineering.   I. Boga, Steve, 1947-   . II. Title.
GV200.C76   1996
796.522—dc20                                              96-8909
                                                              CIP

# Contents

# An Important Note to Readers

This book contains much useful information about the sport of rock climbing. Before engaging in this potentially hazardous sport, however, you must do more than read a book.

The sport requires skill, concentration, physical strength and endurance, proper equipment, knowledge of fundamental principles and techniques, and unwavering commitment to your own safety and that of your companions.

The publisher and authors obviously cannot be responsible for your safety. Because rock climbing entails the risk of serious and even fatal injury, we emphasize that you should not begin climbing except under expert supervision. No book can substitute for proper training and experience under the guidance and supervision of a qualified teacher.

# Introduction

*We never grow tired of each other, the mountain and I.*

—Li Po

The goal of lightweight alpine climbing is to move lightly and efficiently through the mountains without base camps or lines of support, basically as an animal does. The focus is on simplicity, carrying only what is essential, sacrificing creature comforts for mobility. It is to climb as much, as lightly, and as quickly as possible. Very often it means starting while it's still dark. Lightweight alpine climbing demands a willingness to give up some comforts to be able to climb more easily and in some ways more safely.

When I tell nonclimbers that I'm a climber, their two most common responses are risk and fear of heights. People perceive climbing to be a high-risk sport, and they exaggerate the dangers. I picture a scenario that seems pretty typical: Two novices are out on a climb, when a big rock falls about a hundred feet from them. They think, "What if that had hit us? We could've been killed! We gotta get out of here!" On the road home, the driver, fiddling with the tape deck, swerves into oncoming traffic, quickly corrects, and laughs about it. No big deal, he thinks, mostly because he has done this before and feels comfortable with the risk, which is certainly greater than it was in the mountains. Yet with time and patience, he probably could have grown comfortable with the risks of mountain climbing, too.

It's true that climbing does not carry a Good Housekeeping Seal of Safety, but does that mean the risk level is unacceptably high? To figure that, you have to consider how it compares with the risks you tolerate in everyday life. When you factor in things like driving and urban living, climbing rates pretty low.

As for fear of heights, is there anyone who doesn't suffer from it? I think a reasonable fear of heights is an important safeguard. A lack of that protective fear could be a real liability up high.

You have to get used to height. I remember years ago hiking up to the top of a 1,500-foot rock face. As I approached the edge, I had to drop to my stomach and slither. I was still 15 feet from the edge, with no possible way to fall, yet I was already crawling on my belly to see over the edge. Hiking up the low-angle side of the rock made that adjustment harder than it would have been if I had climbed the steep side and gotten used to the exposure gradually. Now, of course, I'm much more used to exposure.

People often ask what I like about mountain climbing. Freedom of movement often comes to mind first. The lighter I go, the freer I am to experience the environment, feelings, sensations. Going light keeps me in touch with the feedback from my body. With a heavy pack, I move farther from my true center. If it is too heavy, I'm just enduring, surviving. The closer you can get to passing through the mountains with next to nothing, in the footsteps of Henry David Thoreau and John Muir, the richer your experience will be.

I also appreciate that climbing is multifaceted. It's not just one thing, but a blend greater than its parts, a spectrum of kinesthetic feedback you get when you are moving smoothly. You're not thinking about it, just reacting instinctively. Your body knows what to do. You're in a rhythm, a zone. And looking around you is exhilarating. From up high, with the cliff falling away at your feet, you can see alpine meadows, gleaming turquoise lakes, the wind spraying jewels first on one side, then the other. And the sunrise in the mountains is glorious, all black overhead until a thin orange band tiptoes onto the eastern horizon. After hundreds of times watching the sun and moon chase each other around the sky, I feel that I have a greater understanding of the way one thing revolves around another. I shy away from labeling climbing a spiritual activity, but for me it is more so than pull-ups.

Even if my day doesn't go quite the way I planned, I try not to lose sight of the ultimate goal: having fun. One time in the Palisades, on the east side of the Sierra, I did seven high peaks in one day. I intended to do more, but because I couldn't get enough water, the altitude began to bother me. I started feeling dizzy and realized it would be stupid to go on. The logical retreat was down a gully, which would quickly lead me to the main trail. But I wasn't in a hurry, just avoiding anything really technical. So I decided to take an alternate route that passed by a lake I'd heard was special. Lounging by that lake, it occurred to me that what had started out as a challenging technical project had turned into a laid-back nature walk. The day had two distinct halves, and both were good.

If you get to the stage where you realize you're going to fail—and we all do—look for another way to make it right. If you can be flexible and change your plans, you're less likely to be reckless.

People wonder how I can climb alone, which I do sometimes. Don't I get lonely? Not really. Perhaps I'm too busy being awed by my surroundings. Even when I go solo, I have two opposing voices inside my head to keep me company. One is devoted to building my confidence, stroking me with praise: "You're fit and strong; you can do anything; you're Superman." The other one goads me to greater effort: "You're not in good enough shape for this; you need to work harder; get off the couch."

**Solo climber on Mount Ranier, Cascade Range.**  LARRY JOHNSON

In the end, I succeed on some climbs and fail on others. But I stretch my limits more by trying new projects than by repeating old ones I'm sure I can do. If I always stayed safely within my comfort zone, I would learn little about my capabilities.

The boundaries of your comfort zone can shift from day to day. Last Thursday you may have climbed brilliantly, and this time you do everything exactly the same but it's not working. Why can't you just mimic Thursday with the same good results? Because climbing offers too many variables, and you're affected by a biorhythmic ebb and flow, powerful and poorly understood. For greater understanding, ask yourself what you did during the past week or two. When was the last time you took a significant amount of time off? Is illness or injury a factor? Preceding your last great effort, what did you do right?

Don't be too analytical; there are going to be good and bad days no matter what you do. I once drove all night from Canada to Washington, getting no sleep. The next night I planned to get up at midnight and traverse the Stuart Range in central Washington, but I couldn't fall asleep. I lay in my bag anguishing over it: "I gotta get to sleep...I gotta get to sleep or I'm in big trouble."

The last time I looked at my watch, it was 11:30. I got up at midnight, so in two nights I'd slept about a half hour. But my energy level on that climb was excellent, and I did everything I wanted to do. The moral is, you can't always predict how you will do.

Just like life itself.

---

Lightweight alpine climbing is not terribly technical, and this book is not going to teach you technical rock and ice climbing. For that information, consult other books in this series, specifically *Free Climbing with John Bachar* and *Ice Climbing with Alex Lowe* (due fall 1997). Use this book to learn how to go light, high, and far.

# − 1 −

# History

*I was fortunate to have the opposite of vertigo, for I found a physical comfort in looking down from great heights.*
—JOHN BUCHAN

Rather than writing a world history of free climbing, which can be found in plenty of other books, I will focus on my own history and how I came to discover lightweight alpine climbing.

I was born in 1958 in eastern Canada. As a kid, I was drawn to adventure. Before I started climbing, I did a lot of hiking with my dad and friends. We scrambled up mountains, but for a long time I did nothing technical. In fact, I had no interest in technical climbing until I read *I Chose to Climb*, by mountaineer Chris Bonington. I tried technical climbing, and suddenly it was all I wanted to do. I was seventeen and ready to devote myself to a new adventure, a new life.

I had dabbled in other sports—track and field, karate—but I didn't like being told when I could play, how long I could play, when I had to stop. Climbing, on the other hand, allowed me to go at my own pace and to do as much or as little as I wanted. And there were so many different facets to it, not just a series of repetitive movements. I was attracted to the calculated boldness, the freedom.

When I started climbing, I knew the dabbling was over. I had found what I wanted to do forever. I teamed up with my friend Richard Suddaby, who had a little climbing experience. We sought out pure climbing—no hiking—close to the road, undiluted by anything else. We became almost fanatical about it.

We read climbing books, but there was no place to take lessons. Not surprisingly, we made mistakes. I read a book by Allen Blackstone until it fell apart in my hands. It was useful, but it touted British techniques that were already out of date. Soon I began to read anything on climbing I could find, from *National Geographic* articles to old library books. Back then I'd listen to anybody; I felt my greatest strength was knowing my own ignorance.

I climbed a lot at Squamish in western Canada, an area that offered big walls and smooth granite. My equipment consisted of the thickest rope I could find—11.5 millimeters—and a heavy, rigid pair of mountain boots with a steel shank, not at all suitable for technical rock climbing. Richard wore running shoes, which in some ways were better, but it was clear that neither was right.

Our first route, a 5.8, offered plenty of adventure. When I tried to navigate the 5.8 part in stiff boots, I went skittering down the slab like a bead of water on a hot frying pan. Picking up speed, I tried to grab the last piece of protection but it burned through my hand. I flew past an overhang before the rope held. I had taken my first 25-foot fall.

I went up again and this time I tried to lasso a tree. But instead of looping the tree, the rope got lodged in some rotten branches. I was too chicken to test it, so Richard did. It was an embarrassing start for me.

We did another climb, a 5.7, which we finished after dark. Some other climbers, seeing "rookie" stamped all over us, waited at the top to help us down. They asked us what routes we had done. We told them about the 5.8, but I was too embarrassed to tell them about my fall. They were impressed that we could do it with the footwear we had on. So my first day of real climbing was also my first day of lying about what I had done.

I climbed a lot that first year. My aspirations were merely to become good enough to be called a climber. I had no visions of greatness, just a desire for the competence necessary to tackle the cliffs without feeling like I was risking disaster at every turn.

Eventually I got into a group of a dozen or so climbers that hung out at Squamish. The weather there is often hideous, and we always figured that held us back. But in some ways it may have been a blessing. Whenever the weather improved, we climbed incessantly, certain that it couldn't last. Climbers in areas like California can be lulled into laziness by the good weather.

Once I started climbing 5.10, which was about as difficult as anyone was doing in Canada, people began telling me how good I was, how I should be doing even more difficult climbs. When you hear that, it feeds your ego, makes you more competitive. But that turned climbing into just another sport. I went on to climb 5.11 and 5.12, but some of the fun had seeped out of it for me.

Then in the early eighties, after I'd been climbing for about eight years, I got away from difficult free climbs and began free-soloing. I started out on familiar 5.7 and 5.8 routes, way below my limit, then moved on to climbs that were new to me. Mostly, I sought out long routes, 1,000 to 2,000 feet high.

All of a sudden, the fun and freshness were back. None of my friends were into soloing, which told me it wasn't just an ego trip. It's hard to feed your ego doing things other people aren't into, especially when they're not even there to watch. Soloing taught me that what *seems* to be the most fun is in fact the best thing to do, whether it's climbing an artificial wall or an 8,000-meter peak. In other words, don't go for what your friends or the latest climbing magazines say is best, but for what you truly feel is best.

I began to visit other climbing areas, for travel was another way to

Free-soloing on a big route: Difficult free climbs are not the only way to challenge a climber's ability.

DON SERL

keep climbing fresh, to move outside my comfort zone. I climbed the granite walls of Yosemite, the mecca of free climbing. In England, I did a lot of soloing on routes I'd never done before, mostly 5.9 and 5.10 classics. Back in Canada, I visited the Bugaboos, a sort of Alpine Yosemite, with glaciers and granite cliffs soaring up to 2,500 feet.

In the Bugaboos, it came to me that because the cliffs are close together, I could do, say, a 2,000-foot route, come down, do a 1,200-foot route, come down, climb another, and so on. I figured I could string together several routes, with the level of difficulty never exceeding 5.10, but enjoying a lot of climbing in one day.

And so in fourteen hours I did four major routes in the Bugaboos, each of which had previously been considered a full-day climb. Tradition had been that if you did a long route, that was all you did that day, no matter what time you finished. The realization that I didn't have to stop was a major breakthrough for me. To come up with the idea of stringing routes together, and then to discover it was possible, was a dream come true. It was like finding out I could fly.

As far as I knew, no one else in Canada had done anything like that, and I'd never heard of it in Yosemite. It was the birth of my lightweight alpine climbing.

That fall I went to Yosemite and in one day did two big climbs, Sentinel Rock and Higher Cathedral Rock, both over 1,000 feet. It reinforced what I had discovered about linking routes.

I started spending lots of time in Yosemite and soon latched on to the idea of climbing El Capitan and Half Dome in one day. People thought I was crazy. "You haven't even done El Cap in one day, much less both," they would say.

The plan was ambitious, but it wasn't crazy. I knew I'd need a partner, and not just any partner—I believed that Yosemite local John Bachar was the best person in the world for this undertaking. The problem was, I didn't know him. I'd seen him around the climbers' campground, knew what he looked like, but figured he had no idea who I was. And I was too intimidated to approach him, mostly because I looked upon him as a god. He had, in my estimation, brought difficult free-soloing to Yosemite, to North America. He had blown everyone away and gained a good deal of his fame by soloing "New Dimensions", a 400-foot 5.11 route, and later "Nabisco Wall", a notch harder at 5.11c. My plan seemed a lot like choosing Michael Jordan for my intramural basketball team.

Then one day I ran into Bachar, and he came right up to me and asked if I wanted to do some easy soloing with him. As soon as we were by ourselves, he asked me if I'd be interested in doing El Capitan and Half Dome in one day. When he asked me that, I think it was the most exhilarating moment of the whole climb. The best climber in the world, at least for that type of challenge, had just approached me and handed me everything I wanted. If I failed, I had nothing to complain about.

In preparation, we soloed some moderate routes together. I knew that John could handle anything, but he probably wanted to check me out. Our compatibility was terrific, both on and off the rock. Of course, I was so filled with admiration for John that he could do no wrong. We did a practice climb of Half Dome because neither of us had ever done it before. It went faster than we expected.

Then John told me to do nothing until our climb two days later. "Lie in your tent, close your eyes, eat a lot," was his advice. That was back before I believed in rest days. "We'll get out of shape in two days," I protested. "How about if I do some easy soloing?"

"No," John insisted. "Even if you can't sleep, lie in your tent and close your eyes. Better to pretend to sleep than to walk around all wired up."

He was right. When the time came, I was bursting with energy, and he was too. And we got stronger and stronger as the day went on, as though climbing were food to us.

We had set our alarm for 11:00 PM and were at the base of El Capitan for a midnight start. We had counted on the moonlight, but it was overcast. It hadn't been overcast in weeks—was it a sign that we should postpone? We were so psyched that delay was unthinkable. We decided to go for it, feeling that we'd come down if we had to.

In a while the clouds cleared, and I remember thinking that was like a test: *Do you really want to go for it?*

About three-quarters of the way up the 3,000-foot wall, I pulled on a flake of rock and it came partway out. There were two parties below us, and if that rock had dislodged, it probably would have killed someone. John, dressed all in white, lurched forward and shoved the rock back in. He moved so quickly, I saw only a white blur. It was like the act of some superhero.

We did the Nose in ten hours. That's pretty fast, but we could have done it faster if I had been as proficient with jumars as John was.

Afterward, we hiked and rappelled back down to the Valley, where John's wife picked us up and drove us toward Half Dome.

On the hike to the base of Half Dome, I felt like I was the stronger hiker. I felt better about having slowed us up before, as I realized that we each had different strengths.

At the base of Half Dome, we were keyed up, feeling fresh and strong. Unfortunately, there were climbers everywhere. We would have to pass seven parties. About 900 feet up the rock, I approached a climber, who said, before I could open my mouth, "You can't pass. No way. You just can't do that up here." John was supposed to take the lead at that point anyway, so I figured I'd let him handle the guy. After all, he was the superhero.

When the guy saw Bachar, his posture changed dramatically. "Oh sure, you can go ahead," he said, all sweetness. The same thing happened again later. Then a third incident occurred that was even more revealing. In the lead, I came upon three Germans eating lunch on a ledge. When they saw me, they came over as far as their ropes would allow, asking, "Are you John Bachar? Are you John Bachar?"

"No," I answered, starting to feel a little disappointed myself. I could not have been as disappointed as the Germans were, however. They slumped back, perking up again when I added, "But John Bachar is about a hundred feet below me. And he's coming up!"

When Bachar reached the Germans, they gave him a hero's welcome. They were in heaven just being on the same ledge with him. And when John asked to pass, they practically tripped over themselves saying yes.

Farther up Half Dome, a thunderstorm roared in on bear paws, drenching us to the bone. But by that time we had so much momentum, nothing could stop us. We topped out about dinnertime, a little more than four hours from bottom to top, still the fastest time ever. We had to pass seven parties, endure rain, and all that after already having done El Cap. It showed that we were indeed getting stronger.

That climb with Bachar was a huge breakthrough for me. It was not so much the notoriety, because John, as the better-known climber, received the lion's share of the credit, as was appropriate. More important for me was the confidence I gained, which has since enabled me to do even more strenuous climbs.

Since John had already done "New Dimensions" and "Nabisco Wall," and I had already soloed the North Face of the Rostrum, the next logical step up was "Astroman." People often ask if I felt competitive with Bachar. Not at all. I was inspired by him. He's too good at what he does. Also, we're into different types of climbs. He loves the shorter routes, and I prefer the longer ones. The Rostrum is about the same rating as "Nabisco," but "Nabisco" and "New Dimensions" are about three pitches long, and the Rostrum is about nine pitches. The idea of doing the next great classic climb was my romantic ideal.

Longer, with more difficult pitches, "Astroman" is definitely a step up from the Rostrum. I had long heard the question in Camp 4: *"Who's going to solo 'Astroman'?"* Whenever it was directed at me, I replied that I wasn't interested. It was my way of diffusing pressure.

Then, in 1987, a year after Bachar and I climbed El Capitan and Half Dome, I soloed "Astroman." It was a classic, the ultimate long, difficult free climb—maybe in the world. Of course, there are other technically difficult free climbs, but because I saw "Astroman" as the ultimate, I was never able to get psyched the same way for the others.

So I turned my attention to long climbs in the mountains. I discovered the magic of the High Sierra, where the weather is more predictable than in Canada or the Rockies, offering incredibly long climbing days. In a typical long day, I would scale a steep buttress, hit a ridge crest, and then stay with the crest as long as I could handle it, always searching for ways to maintain continuous climbing (no hiking). At times, I would traverse an entire minirange. They weren't necessarily the most difficult routes, but it was a dramatic lengthening of the day.

Looking into the future, I intend to keep changing in order to maintain freshness. On the other hand, it's hard to resist the temptation to stay with what has brought me fun and success—long endurance climbs. There are always more long walls to link up in Yosemite. What's more, I plan to keep traveling outside Yosemite, outside the States, anywhere I can find a long ridge traverse.

# – 2 –

# Getting Started

*All climbers are a product of their first few climbs.*
—YVON CHOUINARD

When you're starting out, evaluate your background. You may have come to mountain climbing with a strong hiking background, a strong rock-climbing background, or no strong background at all.

Even if you have a strong outdoor background but little hands-on climbing experience, you will be able to make educated guesses that reduce the risks of climbing. This makes them calculated risks, which are the only type of risks to take.

If your background is hiking, it would be a good idea to get instruction on rock-climbing technique and equipment use. If your background is climbing, it's harder to get advice on camping, backpacking, and meteorology.

If your experience is in short-route crag climbing, you'll need to tone down your technical goals. If you think you're solid on 5.10, go for routes that are 5.7 or less. Rock climbing has many variables, and when you take the sport into the mountains they probably double. In addition to the usual technique and equipment issues, you will have to deal with loose rock, route-finding dilemmas, tempestuous weather, wet rock, snow over rock, and many other situations.

Sometimes the grade in the guidebook doesn't accurately reflect the degree of difficulty you face on the rock. One reason is that guidebooks are sometimes wrong; another is that the pack on your back combined with altitude and route-finding problems can add degrees of difficulty, transforming a 5.7 into, say, a 5.10. It's easier to get off-route in the mountains because climbs are not as well traveled, making it harder to follow other people's chalk trail. In the mountains, there might be only one or two ascents of a route per year. Often I have climbed a route that's supposed to be a classic, only to sign the register at the top and find out I'm the first one up that year.

## Partners

It's a good idea in the beginning to have a partner, although the importance of this depends on your background and the level of difficulty of the climb. If, for example, you have a strong hiking background and face a climb that appears straightforward, you might tackle it alone. But keep in mind that most of the time, climbs are not as straightforward as they seem. You may get to the top and think there's an easy way down the back side—but there isn't. Even when you're experienced, it's easy to get off-route.

It's almost always safer to have a partner. Partners can belay each other, watch each other's backs, be alert for personality changes that might suggest problems, and go for help if one gets hurt.

On the other hand, climbing alone offers incredible freedom. You're the leader of a one-person expedition. And there's one built-in safety factor going solo: you won't go for it unless everything feels just right. When I'm alone, I'm pretty conservative; with someone else along, I might go for it more.

Some climbers have been goaded on by their partners, with bad results. The competitive part of climbing can be either good or bad and is usually a bit of both. An important skill for a mountain climber—whether alone or not—is the ability to admit you're getting out of your depth.

## Equipment

A lot of people know enough to go lighter than they do, but they read too many equipment articles, too many reviews in *Outside* magazine.

Beginners should resist the temptation to go out and buy a vast array of equipment. Outdoor equipment can be expensive and your attachment to the sport may still be tenuous. Buy only necessities at first; acquire other gear gradually. You will probably want to buy your own shoes or boots—secondhand footwear is dicey—but you may be able to borrow your dad's rucksack or your brother's sleeping bag.

When it is time to buy, seek out legitimate mountain shops that employ trained salespeople. Even if the sticker prices are a tad more expensive than at the discount stores, it will be worth it in the long run; they will sell you the right item, not necessarily the most expensive one.

Even though I'm advising you that less is often more, it may be good for beginners to carry more than they think they'll need. For example, if you're going out for a long day, you might want to take something in which to bivouac, just in case.

One thing that improves with experience is your ability to estimate whether you will be able to return in less than a day, or whether a bivouac will be needed. If you might have to spend the night, ask yourself whether you have enough gear, food, and water along.

If you face a big day and don't want to bivouac, don't be afraid to start your climb in the middle of the night. This will also help you beat the afternoon thunderstorms that are common in the mountains. Things seem a little spookier at that hour, but this feeling can be mitigated by a partner.

**Early morning can be a motivating, rewarding, and practical time to begin a climb.**

DON SERL

Starting early also can provide a huge psychological boost. At first light, when you're well under way and looking down at the valley below, you will think, "Wow, I started way down there and I'm already way up here!" No matter what else happens, you've already done a lot.

If, despite your early start, a bivouac is still a strong possibility, consider taking a stove. Hot drinks can make a huge difference on cold mornings and evenings. And if you're at a high elevation, where freezing mornings are possible, you may need a stove to melt snow for water. Other items that gain importance when facing a bivouac are a bivouac sack, food, water, and a fire starter, preferably a lighter.

## Psychology

Some beginners read a few climbing articles and think they know it all. But I was timid at first, and if you're into climbing for the long haul, I advise you to be the same way. If you're new to the mountains, even if you have experience at the local crag or climbing wall, it's important to tone down the difficulty of your first projects. Besides packs and elevation problems, the mountains offer a greater chance of getting lost, or at least misplaced. The hardest mountain climbing I've ever done was tougher than the guidebook suggested, usually because I veered off-route onto something different than I had planned. It's happened to me lots of times, and it's bound to happen to beginners.

# – 3 –

# Equipment

*As I hammered in the last bolt and staggered over the rim,
it was not at all clear to me who was conqueror and who was
conquered: I do recall that El Cap seemed to be in
much better condition than I was.*
—WARREN HARDING, AFTER THE FIRST ASCENT OF EL CAPITAN

Today, many people going out on a two-day climb take more gear than the old-timers used to take on four-day expeditions. The idea seems to be that since equipment is lighter now, we should take more of it.

In order to make intelligent equipment decisions, you must first answer a few questions:

- Where are you going?
- How long will you be out?
- What sort of weather can you expect?
- Will you be bushwhacking?

Some rely on equipment lists drawn up by others. But such equipment lists often include everything imaginable. The list may have been created by someone whose home range is the Cascades, necessitating raingear tough enough to withstand both bushwhacking and torrential downpours. In your mountain range, you may have neither, in which case it makes no sense to carry that kind of equipment. Nowadays, it's possible to carry raingear that packs down to the size of a bagel. Big, heavy raingear may be five times as heavy and bulky.

Some of the lists I see are enormous. Because my list is so basic, I keep it in my head, but you may prefer to write it down, especially in the beginning.

**Short list of gear for beginners**
Clothes:
  socks
  boots or tough running shoes
  light rain jacket
  nylon, cotton stretch pants—should be easy to pull up
    into shorts for wading streams
  super lightweight pile pullover
  pile jacket
Miscellaneous:
  pack
  Sunscreen—strong
  lip stuff—strong
  sunglasses with case
  hat with brim (and chin strap if the hat isn't snug)
  water filter
  2-quart water bottle
  map and compass
  watch
  first aid kit
For snow and ice:
  gaiters
  ice ax
  crampons
For rock:
  rope
  rock shoes
  appropriate rack harness

## Climbing Equipment

**Ropes.** When I travel alone, I usually don't take a rope, though I sometimes do if I expect to rappel or belay myself.

Consider the following when acquiring a rope:
- *Durability.* How tough a rope you need depends on where you'll be climbing. It's much more of an issue in the mountains than it is at your local crag. A natural mountain phenomenon

called frost fracturing (water seeps into cracks, freezes at night, forces rock apart) creates sharp edges everywhere that can easily trash a cheap rope.

- *Size.* Again, what type of climbing will your rope have to endure? If you are going to do a lot of high-angle rock climbing, the minimum diameter you will want is 9.8 to 10 millimeters (mm). Most climbers tackling low-angle, moderate routes use 8.8 to 9mm. Don't take a rope thicker than 10mm. The 11mm ropes are simply too heavy; it doesn't seem as though 1 millimeter should make that much difference, but it does, not only in the extra weight, but also in the rope drag caused by the extra surface area against the rock.

  Unfortunately, some rope companies are inaccurate about the diameter of their ropes, and some 10s are actually closer to 11s. Look for a true 9.8, which is nice and light.

---

Most hard climbing I've done in the mountains could be easily broken into 80-foot pitches. If most of your routes are moderate, a single half-rope (50 meters, 9mm) will do. A doubled 8- or 9-mm rope can work great on harder pitches.

---

- *Length.* If you are doing moderate climbing, short pitches, or both, you can go with a 150- or 165-foot rope. Some people prefer 200-foot (60-meter), or even longer ropes for ice climbs, but for most mountaineering tasks, you simply don't need that much rope.

  If you climb with a partner, you will often do what's called *fourth-classing,* where both climbers are tied in to the rope, moving together, the first one putting in protection and the second taking it out. A 200-foot rope puts more rope against the rock, creating significantly more rope drag for the leader.

  A longer rope does have its advantages: If you're climbing a 2,000-foot face, or ice climbing where speed is of the essence, a longer rope means less down time, less time setting up and dismantling belays. If you are doing moderate, low-angle climbs, however, a longer rope has no advantages.

- *Water resistance.* Get what's called a *dry rope,* which is more expensive but worth it if you're going to be climbing in the mountains and dragging your rope through snow. Dry ropes shed water; other kinds absorb water if dragged through snow and get heavy, which is, once again, a drag. Dry ropes also tend to be more resistant to wear.

**Harness.** As with most of my equipment, I look for lightweight durability in a harness. Mine is forever in contact with snow and ice and rock ledges. But if you spend most of your time on moderate, low-angle rock, and you won't be hanging on the rope a lot, you can tie the rope around your waist and leave your harness at home. A harness takes up a lot of room, so if you don't need it, leave it behind.

In case you have to rappel, you can take along 5/16-inch tubular webbing, which is quite strong but takes up little room in your pack. Use this to rig what's called a diaper seat (Fig 2). Put the sling behind you, bring a strap up between your legs, and clip a carabiner to it. If need be, you can use it as a rappel anchor.

**Carabiners.** Under normal conditions, use lightweight carabiners. If it's very cold or you're doing ice work, use larger biners that you can manipulate wearing gloves or mittens.

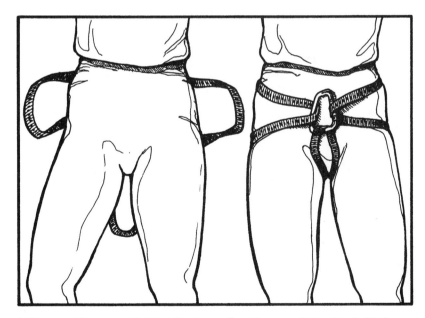

A diaper seat is a compact alternative to carrying a harness. Put a sling behind you, bring a strap up between your legs, and clip a carabiner to it.

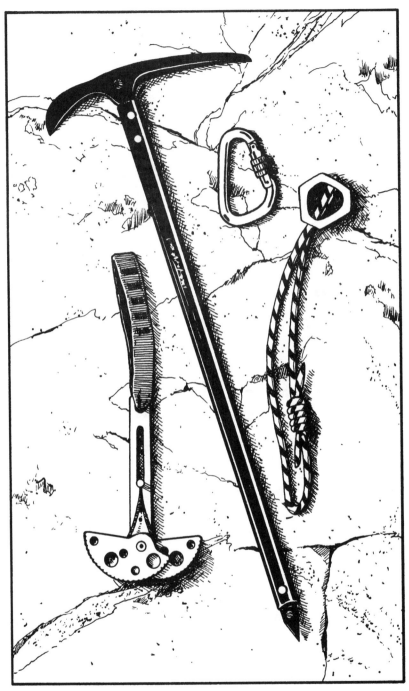

An alpine climber's basic hardware includes SLCDs (spring-loaded camming devices), an ice ax, carabiners, and nuts.

**Pitons, Nuts, and Camming Devices.** I rarely use pitons. They aren't environmentally friendly, and if you take pitons, you must also take a hammer. Instead, I try to climb clean, using nuts and spring-loaded camming devices (SLCDs). I favor nuts, because if you have to rappel and leave them behind, the expense is minimal, whereas SLCDs can cost $50 or more.

**Ice Ax.** People take ice axes far too often. They certainly have their place, but quite often a walking stick will do the job. I usually pick out a sturdy branch on the approach and discard it when I'm done. A sharp rock can serve as an effective step cutter.

If you anticipate a lot of glacier work, as you might in Alaska or the Northwest, you'll need a full-size, big-league ice ax. If you figure to do only occasional ice work, get a smaller one, which you still will be able to use for the important jobs, like cutting steps or plunging into the snow for self-arrest.

## Pack

Unless you're the second coming of John Muir, you will need a pack in which to carry your gear. Up to a point, a daypack will suffice. For bivouacking, cooking, or traversing lots of snow and ice, however, you may need a full-size alpine pack.

When making this important purchase, visit a local mountain shop and talk to knowledgeable salespeople. Ask questions. And keep in mind the following variables:

- *Frame.* For climbing, you need a frameless pack or one with an internal frame. External frames are fine for backpacking, when most of your hiking is on trails, but they are a nightmare for climbing. Even internal-frame packs can be too wide, cramping arm movement. Test this in the store by loading the pack and trying it on.

- *Ease of packing.* The harder a pack is to pack, the easier it is to make mistakes, resulting in an uncomfortable pack.

    Before you pack, consider your goals. If you plan to back-pack into a base camp, drop your big pack, and climb from there with a daypack, you don't have to be as fussy in the way you pack. If, on the other hand, you will be climbing with your alpine pack, arrange things for comfort and convenience. Avoid creating sharp corners that can snag and throw you off-balance. Put soft items—bivy sack, jacket—near your back for cushioning. Place heavy items down low and close to your back, near your center of gravity. If you will be hauling, pad all around the bag to avoid putting holes in it.

## What to look for in a streamlined day pack

medium capacity
sternum strap
compression straps
ice ax loop and strap
padded back
padded shoulder straps
waist strap
easy access pocket for maps, sunscreen, etc.
durability

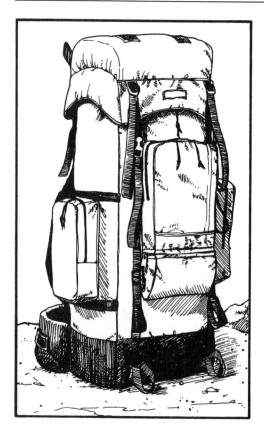

The alpine pack: A mid-size, frameless pack that should be comfortable and durable.

- *Fit.* Be sure that the shoulder straps are long enough to avoid chafing under armpits and hips.
- *Pockets.* Pockets provide easy accessibility for items you might need while climbing, such as maps, water bottle, snacks, insect repellent, or sunscreen. Look for a pocket on the side of the waist strap; this is ideal for a water bottle, enabling you to drink without removing your pack.

---

Being able to reach your water without removing your pack can be more than just a matter of convenience. If you have to take off your pack during a climb in order to get a drink, you may find yourself putting it off, telling yourself, "I'll wait and drink at the top." But because of foreshortening, the top is often farther than it appears, and you may become dehydrated before you make it. That can lead to other problems.

---

- *Straps.* Look for padded straps. Unpadded straps are a misguided attempt to save weight and money. Although padded straps won't seem significant in the first hour, they may seem like the most important thing in the world after eight hours without them.

  If you plan to do much ice and snow, you will need straps for an ice ax and crampons.

  Look for a pack with a sternum strap or shoulder straps that curve toward the center of the chest, to prevent your load from creeping out to the ends of your shoulders. Both types of straps are adjustable, making such packs suitable for different types of activities. When you're climbing, you'll probably want more weight on your shoulders than on your waist; if the weight is on your waist, the pack tends to tip back and forth, throwing off your center of gravity. Later, when you're hiking on the flats, you may prefer more weight on your waist. You should be able to adjust the straps without taking off the pack.

  Straps on the side allow you to compress the pack when it's not full, so that it will protrude just a few inches from your back. This helps keep the weight over your center of gravity. This may not seem important on the approach, but you'll

appreciate it when you hit that first chimney. The more you can flatten your pack against your back, the happier you will be.
- *Reinforcement.* Abrasive rock wears heavily on a pack, so don't try to get by with an ultralight model. Climbing a chimney in a thin nylon pack can rip it out. Instead, get something durable, reinforced in strategic places to withstand the rub of mountain climbing.

## Clothing

**Clothes for Climbing.** In general, you should layer your clothing for warmth and dryness. You can remove layers as you warm up and add them as you cool down. A breathable first layer of long underwear made of lightweight, high-performance polyester, such as Capilene or polypropylene, will provide valuable insulation and wick perspiration away from your body. A waterproof outer shell will protect you from rain or snow. The layers in between should be lightweight, yet provide warmth and breathability.

I usually wear baggy climbing pants of a cotton-nylon blend. They are cooler than tights, and stretchy enough that I can roll them up if I get really hot. I sometimes take polypropylene long-john bottoms for warmth but prefer the feel of cotton T-shirts on top. If you sweat a lot, you may want to wear polypropylene on top, but beware of the odor. A fleece jacket and raingear will provide extra warmth, if needed.

Use high-quality, nylon-wool socks; cotton sport socks soak up water and can cause blisters. I often take along an extra pair.

---

We tend to concentrate on leg muscles, but a long day in the mountains can really tire your feet. Taking a break to wash your feet in a stream and put on clean socks can be rejuvenating.

---

Extra socks can double as mittens on frosty mornings.

---

**Raingear.** I don't always take raingear, but I would recommend it if you are going out for a few days or going into a heavy rain area.

Protecting the upper body is most important—that is, rain jackets are more critical than rain pants. When I'm climbing above treeline in the Sierra, I take lightweight raingear that is only slightly breathable. It weighs so little, and takes up so little room there's no reason to leave it behind. But I don't kid myself—it wouldn't survive five seconds of serious bushwhacking.

In Canada or the Pacific Northwest, where weather and conditions can be severe, I take beefier raingear, tops and bottoms. Look for a breathable coating like Gore-Tex, which can only be applied to heavy-duty raingear. If you plan to hike or climb in the pouring rain, it's an important feature, as it keeps out the rain but allows your perspiration to escape. If it's really coming down though, you'll probably get damp. When you buy Gore-Tex, ask whether the seams have been sealed. Not all have. If they haven't, you can either do it yourself or look for different raingear.

L ook for convenient pocket placement on any serious raingear you buy by putting your pack on over the raingear and testing it.

**Boots.** Boots are your first line of defense against the landscape, where the rubber meets the rock. If you don't have the right footwear, the best equipment in the world won't help.

Assess your needs and determine whether one item can have a dual function. Can you hike and climb in the same shoes? I often wear off-trail running shoes, which are sturdy enough to knock about scree but light enough to wear for hours and hours. I want them form fitting, with very little dead space, but not so tight that going downhill hurts my feet.

Try out your new boots at the local crag before committing them to the mountains. Keep in mind, however, that whatever your ratio, you're not going to be able to climb as hard in the mountains as you can at the crags. For example, I may climb pretty solidly up to 5.8 at the local climbing area in my industrial-strength running shoes, but in the mountains, with a pack and the threat of altitude problems, I may be able to climb only 5.5 in them. So if I'm going to do more difficult routes than that, I take a pair of soft climbing boots. Avoid climbing slippers, which save room but have an inadequate midsole and lack foot support.

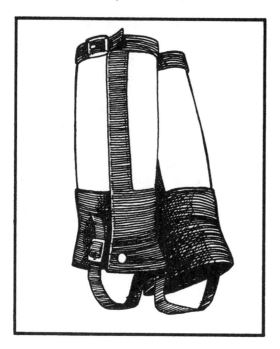

Gaiters keep moisture and cold out of boots and socks, preventing frostbite, blisters, and even hypothermia.

If you have weak or injured ankles, you may need more support than running shoes offer. In any case, right-fitting boots are so critical that you should patronize a mountain shop with knowledgeable salespeople. Avoid mail order unless it is your only option.

If you plan to strap on crampons for snow and ice travel, you will need a stiffer boot. Still, go as simple and light as possible. You can now get boots that weigh a fraction of what they did when I started. Gore-Tex boots are breathable and water repellent.

**Gaiters.** If you think you might be doing much snow travel, take along gaiters, which will help keep snow out of your boots and socks. More than comfort is at stake; if your feet get wet or cold, you are more susceptible to hypothermia and frostbite, as well as blisters.

**Helmet.** The first helmet I had was big and bulky, and I hated it. Helmets today are lighter and more comfortable, but I still don't always take one on climbs. For the last few years, I've concentrated on ridges and buttresses, where rockfall is unlikely. If you plan to spend a lot of time in gullies or on broad faces, it's a good idea to wear a helmet. If you're not sure whether you'll need a helmet, take one along, but keep in mind that it does take up a lot of room.

When buying a helmet, look for a UIAA-approved sticker. Remember that the lighter and more comfortable your helmet, the more likely it is that you'll actually wear it.

## Food and Water

**Food.** I have become a minimalist when it comes to food on climbing trips. I have repeatedly run tests in which I ate little food and had energetic climbing days, and at other times scarfed and bonked. On some of my strongest days, I have consumed little more than water. I am convinced that you shouldn't eat too much, especially not at any one time, lest you become slow and sleepy.

Go for simplicity. Forget about elaborate dinners that need soaking and spices. Consider making sandwiches before you go. My two main culinary concerns are that the food be easily digestible and not radically different from my normal diet.

If you are going out just for a few days, nutrition is not that critical. For such a short time, you can put aside your worries about vitamins and recommended daily allowances. Instead, focus on how closely your wilderness diet conforms to your normal diet. If, for example, you head into the mountains with a rucksack full of energy bars after a lifetime of avoiding them, you can count on getting sick.

When you go out on training runs, start taking the foods you intend to rely on in the mountains. Although you may be able to keep down the occasional PowerBar under stressfree conditions, a steady diet of them while exercising at altitude may have your stomach doing cartwheels. Energy bars work well, but you have to drink lots of water with them or your stomach will get queasy. I use energy bars a lot and never have a problem, but I don't like to go with them exclusively.

If you're going out for just the day, you can include fresh fruit. Because it has a lot of water (read: weight), eat the fruit first. Emphasize fruits with little wasted peel weight, like apples and pears. For a longer trip, rely on dried fruit, keeping in mind that you will have to rehydrate the little suckers.

Got a few ripe bananas? Peel them and stuff them into a wide-mouthed water bottle. Add water and a little powdered milk. When you're in the mountains and in need of a pick-me-up, shake the bottle and voila! Banana smoothy.

I like to take bread. I buy good multigrain bread and don't worry if it gets smashed. If smashed bread bothers you, consider tortillas, pita bread, or bagels.

Sometimes I bake potatoes and take them along—healthy food, no waste. Some people take hard candies, but I don't like them. I do like Fig, Raspberry, and Blueberry Newtons. If you wrap a tortilla around a Blueberry Newton, you have a blueberry crepe.

Some people like to take gorp, a trail munch originally made from peanuts and dried fruit. Gorp once stood for "good ol' raisins and peanuts," but the concoctions today are often laden with chocolate and nuts (read: fat). Fat takes a lot of time and energy to digest—energy you need to climb that next rise. Excess dietary fat is one reason, I think, why people tend to get sick in the mountains. They are pushing their bodies hard while their digestive systems are working overtime to break down that fat. Chocolate and nuts do offer needed calories, but they are hard to digest. Better to go for fewer calories and easier digestibility.

Don't take too much of any one food or your body will rebel. My theory is that the digestive system gets overworked in a specific way and says, "No more!" The most important food tip I can give you is to take a variety of easily digestible, low-fat foods that you like to eat.

Realistically, lack of water is going to hold you back much more than lack of food. Some people like to take Gatorade, but keep in mind that when the carbohydrate level (read: sugar) exceeds about 5 or 6 percent, it actually slows down your absorption of water. You want to get that life-sustaining elixir into your system as quickly as possible, so too sweet a concoction is detrimental.

Cytomax is my favorite sports drink, because it's not too sweet. But usually I go with plain water. For one thing, once you filter for giardia, mountain water is nectar of the gods; second, water is what our bodies crave. If you've ever gone to bed agonizingly thirsty, you know that you dream about water, not Pepsi or Kool-Aid. Water! One time on El Capitan, I went to bed thirsty, woke up thirsty, and then climbed for five hours. Near the top, I found some discarded water bottles and downed a half gallon in a couple of minutes. Now, I don't think I would have been able to drink that much orange juice or soda. But the human body has a great capacity for water.

If you are going out for a few days or just can't go without hot food, take a backpacking stove. Consider freeze-dried meals, which weigh only a few ounces and are quite tasty, especially in the mountains. You can buy them at a backpacking store, but most of your supplies are available at the supermarket. Cocoa, tea, and coffee can supply welcome warmth. Dried soups, which do the same, are lightweight; take along an onion or potato to throw in for a little zip. Other good foods for cooking include oatmeal and rice. Put on some long-cooking rice, bring it to a boil, and turn off the stove, leaving the rice tightly covered. When you return from a long day of climbing, the rice will be cooked.

**A typical water filter and bottle.**

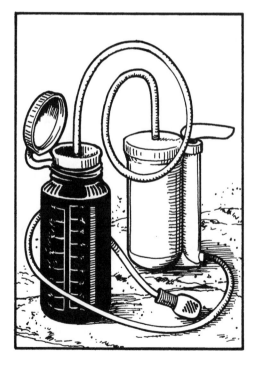

**Water Bottle.** Dehydration is a big problem in the mountains, where the air is dry and you're probably exercising more than usual. If you're going to carry only a quart or two of water, consider Nalgene wide-mouth, high-density polyethylene bottles, which are lightweight and bombproof. I usually carry my water in two 1.7-liter Gatorade bottles, but if you are camping or have limited access to water sources, you might prefer a collapsible gallon jug, which takes up less room when not in use. One brand, Camel Back, has a collapsible bladder incorporated into a daypack; a tube runs from the water supply to your mouth, allowing you to suck water anytime you want. The ultimate in convenience, it's the best choice for long endurance events. Whatever you choose, remember that water weighs more than 2 pounds per quart; carry no more than you need to reach your next water source.

**Water Filter.** Twenty-five years ago you could drink directly from mountain water. Today you run a high risk of contracting giardiasis, caused by the parasite Giardia.

There are three ways the alpine climber can purify water: by boiling, chemical treatment, or filtration. Although boiling is highly effective, it takes a stove, fuel, and time. It also leaves you with hot, flat-tasting water. One strategy is to boil your water just before bedtime, then pour it into drinking bottles. You can use these as hot-water bottles in your sleeping bag. Tighten the tops securely.

For climbers and backpackers, chemical treatment means either Halazone (chlorine) or Aqua Potable (iodine). But chlorine doesn't kill Giardia, and iodine gives the water a ghastly taste, although an additive is now available that neutralizes that.

The best solution is to carry a lightweight, portable filter, the best of which remove not only Giardia but viruses and bacteria, too. There are numerous models, some smaller than your water bottle. Filter pores must be 5 microns or smaller to remove Giardia. Filters can clog, so make sure the one you buy can be easily cleaned or has a replaceable filter. Water filters are fairly expensive, but they last a long time, don't weigh much, and are the best solution to the Giardia problem.

## Camping and Bivouac Gear

To decide whether to take camping gear, consider your plan of attack. If you're going to backpack in and set up a base camp, for example, you may decide to carry a full load, including sleeping bags and tent,

**A bivy sack is more portable and practical than a tent if you're camping alone.**

on the first leg. If you are with other people, a tent is especially nice; alone, a bivy sack may suffice.

If you are uncertain whether you will make it back to camp or car before nightfall, take at least some bivouac gear. A bivy sack weighs so little and offers such peace of mind, it's really an easy call.

## Other Gear

**First-Aid Kit.** I know of a doctor who goes to the mountains and carries only breathable adhesive tape, gauze, painkillers, and antibiotic ointment. He believes those four items will suffice. When I'm mountain climbing, I follow the doctor's advice, except for the gauze. I figure if I ever need gauze, I'll rip up my T-shirt.

As with all pieces of equipment, I consider the odds. If the item in question is something I might need one in a thousand times and it's not lifesaving, I won't take it.

I add a lighter to my emergency kit, in case I need to start a fire. I don't start many, but a fire can save your life, and a disposable lighter weighs next to nothing. Though matches are a great invention, they can get wet.

**Headlamp.** Since I often start before first light, a headlamp is an essential piece of equipment. It serves as a flashlight but leaves your hands free for climbing and other things. Take along an extra bulb and batteries. Halogen bulbs are much brighter and better for climbing but drain the batteries more quickly.

**Swiss Army Knife.** This is a very handy gizmo, capable of performing several tasks, from whittling to opening wine. Such versatility is invaluable—look for it in other equipment.

**Sunglasses.** If you climb above the treeline, surrounded by exposed rock and snow, sunglasses are a necessity. Even on cloudy days, 60 to 80 percent of ultraviolet (UV) light can reach your unprotected eyes. The reflection off those light-colored surfaces can burn your corneas and cause temporary blindness. One time when I was climbing in Alaska, I kept my glasses on while I was on a glacier but took them off so that I could see better while climbing on rock. The next morning, it felt like I had a big splinter in one of my eyes. For a couple of days, I had to cover my bad eye with cotton, then dark glasses, then goggles, to block out all light.  If I go out for more than a day now, I take an extra pair of sunglasses, because if I lose my only pair and become snow-blind, I simply can't climb.

Manufacturers are not required to reveal how much UV protection sunglasses provide, but many do. Look for shades that block 100 percent of UV light and, unless you plan to cross a glacier, transmit 75 to 90 percent of visible light. Polycarbonate (plastic) lenses are lighter, cheaper, and shatterproof. On the other hand, glass is more scratch resistant, accepts antireflective coatings, and offers greater clarity. Consider photochromic lenses, which darken with increased visible light.  If you're going to spend a lot of time on ice or snow, look for sunglasses with side blinders.

If you lose your sunglasses while climbing, you can make temporary ones by cutting slits in two pieces of cardboard.

**Sunblock.** This is especially important at high altitudes, where the atmosphere is thinner and the reflection from rock and snow can be punishing.

**Insect Repellent.**  This can be an important creature comfort, especially if you're camping. I've been to places where the mosquitoes were so bad, my only escape was to run. Repellent won't keep them from buzzing you, but it will prevent them from biting you. A non-aerosol repellent weighs so little, there's no good reason not to take it.

**Map and Compass.** If you're traveling through unfamiliar country, a topographical map and compass can be valuable. You can find both at the local backpacking store. Both items are lightweight, so if you're in doubt, take them along. In the Sierra, I usually take a topographical map, but don't always take a compass. In places like the Cascades and the Rockies, where weather fronts can strike with little warning, sometimes creating a roiling whiteout, a compass can be a lifesaver.

A map is useful in many ways. If the altitude is bothering me and I decide to quit early, I can consult my map for a reasonable escape route. By examining the distance between contour lines and other features, I can determine whether the drainage I intend to navigate is gradual or eventually turns into a cliff that will force me to climb back up again.

At first glance, a topographical map may look like an incomprehensible jumble of squiggly lines, but it's really quite legible. Here are a few things you need to know about topo maps:

- The thin contour lines are called *intermediate contours,* and the bold ones *index contours.* Every fifth contour is an index contour, and its elevation is noted periodically along its length. To determine which way the ground is sloping at a particular spot, follow the two closest index contours with your finger until you find their elevations. Once you know which way the ground is sloping, you can tell whether the nearby V's or U's represent a valley or a ridge.

- The vertical distance between contour lines—the *contour interval*—is always given. If the contour interval is 20 feet, you climb or drop 20 feet if you travel from one line to the next. The larger the contour interval, the less detailed the map. The contour interval varies from map to map but is always the same on a given map. A map of the flatlands of Florida might use a contour interval of 10 feet; in the Rocky Mountains, it might be 100 feet.

- To calculate your gain or loss of elevation, count the number of contour lines you cross and multiply by the contour interval. For example, if the contour interval is 100 feet and your route up the mountain crosses nine lines, you have gained approximately 900 vertical feet.

- Lines close to one another indicate steep terrain—an abrupt drop, falls, or a canyon—whereas lines that are far apart show

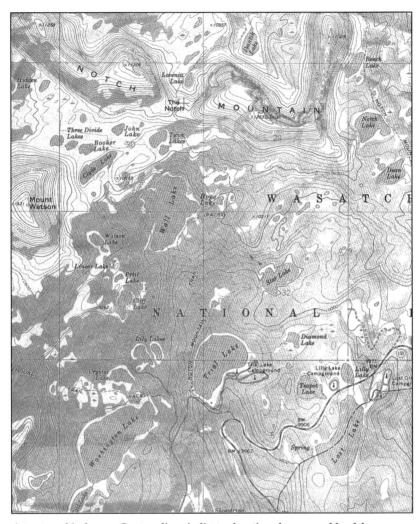

**A topographical map. Contour lines indicate elevation changes and land formations. Lines close to each other indicate steep terrain. An X notes the actual height of specific objects, such as mountain peaks and settlements.**

a gradual change in elevation. Because a vertical cliff has an elevation change over nearly zero horizontal distance, mapmakers depict such cliffs with merging contour lines.

- If you walk along a single contour line, you will remain at the same elevation.
- The closed end of contour V's point upstream.

- U-shaped contours indicate an outjutting ridge of a hill or mountain. The closed ends of the U's point downhill.
- The actual height of many objects—mountain peaks, settlements, trail junctions—is often noted, usually with an X.

The simplest way to use a map to determine which direction to go is by orienting it. Inspect both the map and your surroundings, then twist the map until it corresponds to the terrain. Once accomplished, the map is oriented.

If you can't line up terrain features with map features, you may need a compass. Whole books have been written on land navigation, but you can learn the basics in about thirty minutes. Before you start, make sure you are holding the compass properly. Cradle the baseplate in your right hand, and frame the dial with the thumb and forefinger of your left hand. Tuck your forearms firmly but gently against your body to create a secure triangle, the apex of which is the compass. Position the compass just above your navel, right along the midline of your body, about 6 inches away from your stomach.

Now determine which end of the needle points north. It is usually painted red. Keeping the compass flat, move it until this end of the needle points to the N. You have located north, and from this you can determine the other three directions.

An inexpensive floating-dial compass will suffice on well-marked trails or in familiar country. But even semiserious navigation demands an inexpensive orienteering compass with movable dial and transparent base. An orienteering compass has several advantages:

- You can determine your bearings from a map without a separate protractor and without having to orient the map to north. This means that it is easy to figure your bearing while shuffling through nature. And it's so simple that an eight-year-old can learn its basics in minutes.
- Your direction of travel (bearing) is locked onto the compass dial. There's nothing to memorize or write down.
- The ruled scale along the edge of the plastic baseplate makes it easy to figure map distances.
- Liquid-damped needles reduce oscillation in seconds.
- The system works down to minus 40 degrees F.

An orienteering compass has two basic parts: a transparent plastic baseplate which has various scales along its edges, and a housing,

Knowing how to use an orienteering compass makes navigation easier.

Don Geary

which is mounted on the baseplate so that it can be easily rotated. The bottom of the housing is transparent.

Within the housing are a magnetic needle, north arrow, and direction-of-travel arrow. The painted end of the magnetic needle always points north, so long as you keep your compass away from iron objects. The north arrow is usually a red arrow at the bottom of the housing. The lines parallel to this arrow are called north-south lines. The direction-of-travel arrow, the auxiliary direction lines, and the longer edges of the baseplate serve as direction lines.

Because an orienteering compass is also a protractor, you can sight a landmark in the field and take its bearing. This is simply the measure of the angle between two lines, one pointing north from your position and one pointing toward the landmark. Taking a bearing in the field is a simple three-step procedure.

1. Point the direction-of-travel arrow at the landmark. Hold the compass level so that the needle swings freely.
2. With the baseplate still, rotate the housing until the N on the dial points to the painted end of the needle.
3. Read the bearing at the direction of travel arrow. You can keep the

dial set to this number, although it's good to keep it in mind as well.

A more accurate way of taking and following a bearing is to use map and compass together.

1. Place the compass on the map and align the direction-of-travel lines on the baseplate so that both your present location and your destination lie along one long edge of the baseplate, and the direction-of-travel arrow is pointed toward your destination.

2. Turn the compass housing until its north-south lines align with the north-south lines (meridians) of the map. Make sure the north end of the compass lines (*not* the needle) corresponds to the north end of the meridian lines. When all that is set, read the bearing where the direction-of-travel line meets the dial.

3. Hold the compass level in front of your body. Turn your body until the red end of the needle is pointing toward the north end of the housing lines. Follow the direction-of-travel arrow to your destination.

---

To count degrees, start at the north line (0 degrees) and go clockwise around the compass dial. An object due east has a bearing of 90 degrees relative to your position; one due south is 180 degrees; and one due west is 270 degrees.

---

When buying equipment, you seldom need to buy the most expensive items. My favorite water filter, for example, is one of the cheapest. The same may be true for your boots or bottles. The most expensive item can often be too bulky, but on the other hand, you probably don't want the cheapest version, either. Assess your needs, always keeping in mind that gear—no matter how new and expensive—can get broken, lost, or ripped off.

---

**Watch.** Sometimes it's the little things that make a difference. A watch with an alarm and a luminous dial can be important for that 3:00 AM wakeup call. And if you know that thunderstorms roll in around 2:00 every afternoon, a watch will help you know when to turn back.

Avocet watches have the above features, plus an amazingly reliable altimeter and barometer. They are temperature compensated and adjust nicely to atmospheric changes.

## Conclusion

I choose climbing objectives that are technical, but not so technical that they slow me dramatically. Accordingly, I seek an equipment load that allows me to move quickly. If I'm not sure about an item, I tend to leave it behind. Of course, I must then be prepared to retreat if things get too dicey. It's a price I'm willing to pay for having a more enjoyable time. If I do have to turn around, I have the satisfaction of knowing that I've had a great time up to that point.

When evaluating whether to take a piece of equipment, ask yourself, "If I don't take this, am I merely going to be inconvenienced and uncomfortable, or is there a real chance I'll have to be rescued?" Consider not only your own safety, but that of any possible rescuers.

---

## Weight Chart Comparison

| Lightweight Climber | | Heavyweight Climber | |
|---|---|---|---|
| 8mm rope | 5 lbs. | 10mm rope | .7 lbs. |
| webbing harness | 1/2 lb. | normal harness | 1 1/2 lbs. |
| rain jacket for warmth | 0 | extra sweater | 1 1/2 lbs. |
| walking stick & rock | 0 | ice ax | 2 lbs. |
| small pack | 1 lb. | bigger pack | 2 1/2 lbs. |
| light rain jacket | 1/2 lb. | bigger jacket | 1 1/2 lbs. |
| Total | 7 lbs. | Total | 16 lbs. |

---

It's unwise to generalize too much about what climbing equipment others should carry. It depends on the skill of the climber, the difficulty of the climb, the weather, and a host of other factors. If conditions demanded the maximum, I would take the following:

- 8 to 10 slings. Because of frost fracturing, you can use more slings in the mountains. Although most are 5 feet of material, it's good to have a couple of ten-footers along. It's hard to go overboard on slings.

- A cordelette. This is about 20 feet of 7-millimeter rope tied in a loop with a fisherman's knot. You can throw it over a boulder and create an anchor, or use it to equalize existing anchors.
- 6 stoppers. From 1/4 to 1 inch.
- 3 camming devices. From 1 1/2 to 3 inches.
- 12 carabiners
- 1 or 2 ropes. I take a second rope if I need a separate haulbag or if I am doing a big route and I'm not sure if I will make it. The second rope adds peace of mind if you have to retreat by rappel.
- Ice ax and crampons. If you will face only a small snowfield, you can probably leave the ice gear behind and use a rock to cut steps if necessary. For a little larger icefield, you might need a small ice ax. Don't carry a full-size ax and crampons unless absolutely necessary. Crampons will require heavy boots as well.

Create a cordelette by using a fisherman's knot to tie a loop in a rope.

# — 4 —

# Technique

*Security is mostly a superstition. Avoiding danger is no safer in the long run than outright exposure. Life is either a daring adventure or nothing.*

—HELEN KELLER

In order to enjoy lightweight alpine climbing, you have to learn to get by with as little as possible. Reading classic climbing literature reveals that climbers of yore went extremely light. They wanted a light pack (remember, gear weighed more back then) and they were willing to be a little more uncomfortable to achieve that. For warmth, they might take only wool pants and a down jacket, and, yes, they shivered through some nights. Ah, but those glorious days! They loved climbing and were willing to suffer some discomforts in the pursuit of it.

Today, many people go out expecting everything to be perfect. They want hot meals and eight hours of sleep. And so they carry too much weight. Their philosophy seems to be "We probably won't have to bivouac, but just in case we do, we'll take all this extra stuff."

## Preliminaries
Before you drive 200 miles to discover that the climb you seek is closed because of peregrine falcon nesting, do some research. Read guidebooks, which, besides summarizing the climb, will highlight special problems, like mosquitoes, weather, or rockfall. Guidebooks can be wrong or become outdated, so follow up by contacting mountain shops in that area. They can provide sound advice and direct you toward other people to contact, such as local guides.

If you want to hire a guide, ask around rather than just relying on a brochure. Some guides are highly qualified but are jerks; others may be slightly less qualified but are fun to be around.

Scenic routes can be found at any skill level.                    DON SERL

If you're heading for a state or national park, contact rangers for advice and to find out what's off-limits.

You can ask other climbers about a climb, but some have a tendency to sandbag—to rate a route easier than it really is. Rangers and mountain shops are more objective.

In selecting a route appropriate for your skill level, be conservative in the mountains, where variables abound. If you're a 5.7 climber on rock but a beginner in the mountains, start well below 5.7. And do what you prefer—you're bound to be better at it. I like ridges and buttresses, which are more spectacular and less dangerous than gullies. I revel in the expansive views, the feeling of freedom. The farther away from caving, the better for me. Be conservative in your planning at first, and before you head out the door let someone know where you're going and when you'll be back. When you're in the mountains, continually scope the situation for objective dangers and escape routes.

## Pacing

Avoid the sprint mentality when you're mountain climbing. Think of the big picture, the whole climb. When you start, go slower than you think you can, which will help you avoid tweaking those cold muscles. A slow warm-up is the best way to get the most out of your body and to assure a full climbing day without burning out. Go too hard too fast and you won't have a good day, no matter how much you rest after that.

I once did an ambitious traverse with a friend who was in great aerobic shape. He pulled ahead early and I had to ask him to slow down. He was surprised. He knew I did a lot of climbing and thought I'd be leaving *him* behind. But after we were done, he understood. He told me he was amazed that halfway through the climb I was still going at the same pace. In fact, fifteen hours after we started, I was still going at the same pace.

## Route Finding

An important difference between mountain climbing and rock climbing is that mountain climbers do not seek the route that offers maximum difficulty. Instead, the goal is to cover a lot of ground quickly, so you don't want to be hung up in any one place too long.

If you are uncertain, ask yourself which way you would choose if you were doing a first ascent. That will usually sort it out for you. If your guidebook offers information that directly contradicts what you perceive to be the truth, the book may be wrong, or at least so vague as to be useless.

## Protection

Although this is not a technical rock-climbing book, I should say some-

In the appropriate situation, weaving the rope between fractures or trees can be quicker than stopping to place protection.

thing about setting protection. In deciding when to anchor, use the comfort criterion. If you're feeling uncomfortable without protection, then put it in. Look ahead. Don't wait until you're terrified; have it ready to go in case things get tougher. Moreover, if you are going slower because you are unprotected, then put it in.

Again, be more conservative in the mountains. If you take a fall, the ground is likely to be jaggedly uneven and you are probably a long way from help.

Here's a time-saving tip: Instead of stopping to place protection, weave the rope from side to side as you ascend. If you should fall, the rope will snag over a fractured slab of rock and stop your fall. If you go up a cliff with a well-placed tree, you can go up the right side of the tree, then veer to the left. If you fall, the rope will snag on the tree.

You can also save time in this way: When you reach a big ledge, yell, "Off belay!" as soon as you're settled and safe, then put in your anchor. Putting in the anchor before releasing the belayer is time-consuming, and over an entire day it may make the difference between beating a storm and not.

## Chimneys

Chimneys, which are usually secure, offer an obvious way up a mountain. But problems can arise when you wear a pack. If the chimney is easy, you may be able to keep the pack on your back; often, however, it is best to wear it in front with the straps behind you.

If the chimney is too narrow to accommodate the width of both body and pack, you can clip a long sling to your harness and attach your pack to the sling so that it hangs down below your feet. This is a drag, literally and figuratively, but it may give you the room you need in a medium chimney.

## Jamming

If jamming—wedging fingers, hand, fist, or feet into a crack to create an anchor point—feels awkward without a pack, it's going to feel even worse with a pack, especially thumb-down jamming. Try to emphasize thumb-up jamming. At first it may feel insecure, but with practice you will grow used to it.

## Laybacking and Hand Traversing

Laybacking and hand traversing are both strenuous, so plan out your moves ahead of time, and then go full steam ahead to your rest point.

Chimneying with a pack: The pack is attached to a long sling that is clipped on to the harness. The pack should hang down below the climber's feet.

Don't go halfway and then hesitate, wondering whether your arms are going to fail, because then they probably will. Instead, climb steadily and with confidence. This may seem obvious, but many climbers are defeated by that hesitation.

## Cracks

The best crack systems to climb in the mountains are corner systems. Your pack won't get in the way, and you can bridge out with your feet and lean in, so that your weight stays above your feet. Remember, the more you can get your feet to do the work, the longer you can endure. All other things being equal, bridging is the least strenuous way to climb a steep section of rock.

## Downclimbing

Downclimbing is a good skill to practice on your local crags. People tend to think that climbing down is harder than climbing up, but that's mostly because they spend 99 percent of their practice time going up and 1 percent going down. By working at it, you can greatly improve your downclimbing.

Running up hills will strengthen the muscles around your knees so that when you are downclimbing, those muscles will help control the footfall, softening the smack of foot against ground.

Neoprene knee braces can provide support when doing descents. Some climbers wear them around their socks on the way up, then pull them up to support their knees during descent. This reduces the chances of a knee injury.

If you are downclimbing a section with ledges, you may be able to toss your pack from ledge to ledge as you go. Be sure it is packed so that breakables, such as sunglasses, are protected.

## Rappeling

If your only reason for carrying a rope is to rappel, you don't need an elaborate harness. Instead, take 10 feet of 5/16-inch webbing and make a diaper sling. Or do a body rappel, which is uncomfortable but usually feasible. In the mountains, you can often create a rappel anchor by placing a sling over a horn of rock. Be sure to double-check the stability of any horn; if you have any doubts about its stability, back it up with an additional anchor.

Create a rappel anchor by placing a sling over a horn of rock lasso-style.

## Partners

When you climb with partners, it's important to communicate and to be flexible. Jointly consider options, degrees of difficulty, and risks. Your partner is a teammate, not just someone to hold your rope for you.

If I have a strong gut feeling that I shouldn't go for something, I don't go. Consequently, if my partner has such a feeling, I take it seriously. Often there's a good reason for that impulse. Later in the day someone may get sick or the weather may turn bad.

One time in the Bugaboos in Canada, I was psyched to do a certain climb. Fit and raring to go, I was hiking the approach with a friend when I began to feel queasy. An inner dialogue raged within me:

"I really want to do this climb, but..."

"No buts. We're so close, we've got all the gear, the weather's looking good, and it's the last available day to do the climb."

"But I just feel weird."

"Weird? You want to end this because you feel weird?"

I waited a bit to see if the feeling would pass, but in the end, I decided not to go for it. We hiked back to the hut and I was feeling fine, wondering whether I'd made the right decision. But then all of a sudden, a horrendous storm moved in. Lightning was hitting everywhere. Even if we had been retreating at that point, hiking across the glacier would have been miserable, and maybe worse.

As you gain experience, you refine the instincts that help you get a fix on what feels right and what doesn't. Monitor those instincts; pay attention to them. It's easy to tell yourself to listen to your body, but consider the following scenario:

You're facing an early-morning alpine start, and it's cold, dark, and intimidating outside the tent, and contrastingly warm and comfortable inside your sleeping bag. It's easy to trick yourself into believing the loudest voice, which is saying, "This doesn't feel right. I think we should stay in bed." Don't be seduced by the tendency of a body at rest to want to stay at rest.

It is seldom just one factor that makes it right or wrong to continue. You must constantly ask the question: "Are we reckless to push on, or are we being superstitious or spooked?"

If you do turn around, avoid thinking of your trip as a failure. Try to gain sustenance from the whole experience, not just the summit. My favorite time on a long climb is about the halfway point. By then I've warmed up, I'm in an exhilarating place, starting to cruise, but it's not nearly over. Near the end, I'm sad that I'm almost done.

A lot of partnerships are ruined by success. The individual climbers are told how great they are, and it doesn't take long before they believe it. One climber inevitably gets more credit than the other for their mutual accomplishments. Resentment builds, then festers.

But when a partnership is strong, and both climbers are capable and compatible, it's a wonderful feeling. If it works out with a best friend, that's a bonus. But beware: Sharing an incredibly intense adventure can make or break a relationship.

---

Be wary of trying to coax your spouse or mate to climb with you. Couples who climb together often bicker together. My girlfriend Karine and I do very well climbing together, but that's pretty unusual.

# – 5 –

# Training

*Every step (in mountaineering) is a debate between what you are and what you might become.*

—GEORGE MEREDITH

If you get even remotely serious about mountain climbing, you may want to work out away from the mountains. When devising a training schedule, keep in mind that in both hiking and mountain climbing, most of the work is done by the legs, and that's the main area of the body to train. Do a lot of climbing, of course, but mix in other kinds of mostly lower-body exercise.

The most important physical quality a mountain climber can have is endurance. For rock climbing, strength is paramount, but when you're linking long routes together, you need the endurance that enables you to go for several hours.

The most basic and beneficial way to train the legs and increase endurance is by running, and running uphill is the least punishing on the joints. The uphill feet don't travel as far with each step and therefore don't strike the ground as hard, and because you are fighting gravity, you are forced to go slower. That makes uphills fairly benign on feet, ankles, knees, and hips. Downhill, in contrast, is harder on all those joints.

Accordingly, the core of my training program is running up hills and walking down hills. The focus is not sprinting, but big hills and steep trails. A workout like that is more difficult than running or bicycling the flats, the aerobic choice of many people. I try to redline it— that is, go at a fast pace, but one that I can maintain for thirty to sixty minutes. On a steep trail, an hour is quite a workout.

CHRIS FALKENSTEIN

**An uphill run strengthens the legs and increases endurance, and less joint stress occurs than in running downhill or on level ground.**

After that strenuous hour, you can cruise downhill at a more relaxed pace. It's a wonderful time to cool down, enjoy nature, solve problems, daydream, or simply clear the mind.

Some days you aren't going to feel as strong as others. The reason could be physical, so listen to your body. Take your pulse or use a heart-rate monitor to check for abnormalities. If your heart rate is elevated, you should probably lighten the workout that day. But often the problem is more psychological than physical. If it's merely a matter of not feeling like going for a run, I usually force myself to go. I start slowly, giving it a fair chance, and if after ten minutes I still feel bad, I quit. But usually after ten minutes, I feel pretty good.

It's critical to take the first step. The mind is lazier than the body, and if you give in too easily, you'll never get off the couch. Besides, much of the time, a good workout is exactly what the doctor would have ordered for what ails you. I usually feel better at the end of a run than at the beginning.

Creating a weekly training schedule has merit, but you should keep it flexible enough to allow for your biorhythmic peaks and valleys. If, for example, you feel like Frank Shorter on Tuesday, a scheduled slow day, consider going hard that day. Conversely, if you feel rotten on a supposedly hard day, be flexible enough to back off and go easy. The best way to gauge how hard to go is to apply the fun test: After the warmup phase is over, ask yourself whether you're having fun or are counting the minutes until it's over.

If you're just starting to run, you probably won't like it all that much. At first, the effort is considerable and the results undetectable. But if you make the commitment to begin, build slowly, and stay with it, two things will happen: You will start to see results in both performance and appearance, and you will start to enjoy it. Once you establish and adhere to a training program, you will begin to look forward to your workouts. Either that or you will find other ways to spend your time.

Although you should battle through inertia—the tendency of a body at rest to stay that way—scheduled rest days are critical. Some climbers like to believe that they are exceptions to the rules of exercise physiology, but the rules apply to everyone. People are different in many ways, but the basic principles of overexertion and rest are the same.

## Power Training

I don't believe that power workouts help that much for mountain climbing. Reinhold Messner, probably the greatest mountain climber who ever lived, had an exhausting routine that included massive hill runs and back-and-forth traverses of the wall of a farm building, but very little power training. Messner believed, rightly in my estimation, that a mountain climber's time could be better spent on activities other than lifting weights.

One reason for that is the nature of the sport. The hardest mountain climb I know of in the Sierra is 5.12a, much easier than the hardest rock climb. The average difficult free climb in the mountains is probably about 5.10, so mountain climbers are rarely faced with really daunting power moves. Because they have a lot of ground to cover and often need to finish before the snow softens or the afternoon thunderstorms roll in, speed is more of an issue than power.

Having said that, however, no climber should completely ignore strength training. Gym workouts can be useful, especially if you can't get to the mountains. I once went through a period of several weeks when I was working and had no time to climb. I visited the gym every morning, concentrating on doing a variety of pulling exercises. (I avoid doing a lot of pull-ups as it often leads to tendinitis.) I did lots of repetitions, approaching, but not reaching, failure, with low weight and little rest in between the different types of pulls.

M uscles get stronger from doing fewer reps with heavier weights, and tendons get stronger from lots of low-weight reps.

After six weeks, when I finally went climbing, I found I had great strength and endurance. I could climb all day and wasn't sore the next day. If I had it to do over again, I'd make only two changes in the program. I'd increase the intensity—including maybe one power workout a week in which I'd go right to failure—and add rest days. An intense power workout may leave you so cooked that you can't do your job, however, even if it's just pushing a pencil.

A true power workout emphasizes more weight and fewer reps. Many climbers do weighted pull-ups, adding more and more weight around their waists. An alternative is to work out on a lat-pull machine. Even though pulling is more important than pushing for climbers, ignoring the opposing muscles will cause you to develop an imbalance.

## Stretching

I do almost no passive stretching, the kind where you sink into a stretch and hold it for several seconds. Instead, I favor dynamic stretching—that is, slowly raising and lowering the limbs. For example, I might do ten leg lifts with my left, then ten with my right, always lowering the leg with control.

Unlike passive stretching, which does not get the blood surging through the extremities, dynamic stretching is a good warm-up for cold muscles. It also helps you gain strength in the areas being stretched. I saw benefits two weeks after I began dynamic stretching. It has allowed me to gain maximum flexibility faster, maybe in five minutes instead of twenty. Simple, easy, with no equipment required, it permits a maximum range of flexibility for the rest of the day.

## Bouldering

Bouldering is ropeless, solo climbing usually done within jumping distance of the ground. It allows you to try moves over and over without fear of falling very far. For that reason, you can be relaxed, think positively, and push yourself. With a little imagination, bouldering can be done anywhere there's a rock or a building. The one rule is: Don't climb higher than you're willing to fall.

Although bouldering is best for working on the intense power moves of rock climbing, it can also serve a purpose for mountain climbers. With the right boulder, you can traverse back and forth, say, 30 feet one way and 30 feet back, as many times as you want. In this way, the focus shifts from intensity to endurance. Beware, though, bouldering can be so much fun that you may decide to blow off this week's big north face.

You can do tougher moves on boulders than you can high up on a rock face. Starting fresh from the ground, you can do moves you'd never do after even 50 feet of climbing. The hardest single moves in the world have all been done on boulders; after all, if you're obsessed with doing a boulder problem, you can conceivably try it hundreds or thousands of times over many years. Although it can be productive to go

**Bouldering on large rocks improves strength and is good practice for difficult climbing moves.**

CHRIS FALKENSTEIN

bouldering by yourself, it's usually better to go with other people, especially when you're starting out. If you are doing difficult or awkward boulder problems, you would be wise to have a spotter. Can't find a boulder? Try a stone wall.

Bouldering success can provide the confidence you need to succeed high up on a rock face. If you can do all the boulder problems in your area, it will give you a huge psychological boost when you're mountain climbing. A lot of people skip bouldering, but I believe that's a mistake. It really is the best way to develop the confidence needed to carry you up the rock.

## Mental Training

Before I even knew the terms, I used both visualization and positive thinking to toughen and psych myself mentally. While you're training, visualize yourself doing exactly what you're training for. See yourself moving well, surging with confidence.

For example, if I'm doing a hill run, I don't daydream. I see myself in the mountains getting stronger. Then, when I'm actually in the mountains, there is a positive carryover. The time to daydream is later, when you are walking downhill.

It's important to maintain a positive attitude during training. Tell yourself how much fun you are having. If you can push yourself, but not so hard that it spills over into agony, it's amazing how much more fun training becomes. By focusing on that killer sunrise, those breathtaking vistas, you can trick yourself into feeling happier.

After a morning workout, when I come back down and see my friends just waking up, I have this feeling that I've just gotten away with something, that I've enjoyed something they're not going to have.

Before hearing of visualization I used it to prepare for my solo climb of "Astroman." I walked into a clearing by the Merced River where I could peer through the forest and see the route, all 1,500 feet of it. I saw myself walking up through the talus, getting to the base, climbing the different pitches all the way to the top; I saw myself walking along the rim, down a gully, and back to the base. Then I would do it again, over and over, never sloppy or scared, always smooth, strong, and confident. Visualization of success eventually spilled over into the climb itself.

If you go through an extended period when you just can't muster the positive energy necessary to succeed, it's probably time to take a break. I once had extreme, prolonged burnout. It was the same year I climbed El Capitan and Half Dome with John Bachar. I had what seemed like ambitious plans for that year, and I met all my goals. People said to me, "Oh, you did everything you wanted to do. You must be so excited."

But you have to be careful what you wish for—you just might get it. Once that happened, I had nothing to shoot for. No challenges. The result was an apathetic layabout. I couldn't work out. I would run a half mile and have to quit. If I could have tested my muscle strength and lung capacity, I believe they would have been fine. But I was psychologically incapable of working hard.

After a three-month hiatus, I came back stronger than ever. I attribute it to the burnout, followed by a layoff with no climbing. After all, no professional athlete tries to stay in top shape all year round.

## Cool-down

The cool-down is an important final phase of exercise during which the rate of physical exertion, and hence the heartbeat, is gradually decreased. How thorough and effective your postworkout cool-down is depends a lot on what your workout was.

If, for example, you go hard in the mountains for eight or twelve hours, you aren't going to return to the car and do cool-down exercises. It's simply not going to happen. But after a gym workout, you can go for an easy swim or a bike ride, not for its workout value but for its cool-down value. Or you can park your car a ways from the gym and walk to it when you're done.

If you're climbing or running uphill, the perfect cool-down is to walk downhill. That will save your knees, give you time to reflect, and allow you to recover gradually from your workout.

## Diet

Eat small meals and limit your fat. Big meals will make you feel lethargic; fat takes time, energy, and water to digest. I've had huge days—15,000 feet of elevation gain, eighty pitches—on less than 1,000 calories. One time, while climbing for six days in Washington, I averaged twenty-five pitches and 700 calories a day. Each morning I was sluggish for the first half hour, but if I pushed through that, I could climb all day. I did a traverse in seventeen hours that some expected to take five days—all on six Fig Newtons. It was not a conclusive scientific test, but it convinced me that less can indeed be more.

Of course, everyone has different metabolic constraints. My girlfriend, who is very lean, has to eat often and a lot. Run your own tests and discover what works for you.

## Training Tips

In summary, here are some of the best training tips, whatever your sport:

- *Specificity of training.* Because you reap what you sow, imitate as much as possible what you intend to do. Use long workouts to increase endurance, and short, fast workouts to increase speed.
- *Training edge.* Workouts stress the body. By training hard, the body adapts to that stress and eventually performs better.
- *Rest as recovery.* John Bachar taught me that less can be more. Don't be afraid to take several rest days to allow the body to adapt to the stress of exercise.
- *Hard days, easy days.* Alternating hard and easy days permits recovery from the rigors of going hard every day.
- *Tapering.* To restore life to tired legs, reduce your output as a big climb approaches.
- *Peaking.* This is hard-easy taken to a seasonal level. Because no one can stay in peak form all year long, schedule alternate seasons of peak training and relaxed training.
- *Listening to your body.* Perceived exertion is real exertion. The pace that feels right is right.
- *Stretching.* Running, walking, and backpacking cause leg muscles to grow tight and lose flexibility. Do stretches to counter this.
- *Strengthening.* Hikers, climbers, and runners often suffer from muscle imbalances. Muscles at the front of the leg overpower those in back; muscles of the upper body are weaker than those of the lower body. To compensate, do exercises for general fitness and consider cross-training.
- *Carbo Loading.* For maximum energy, carbohydrates and some protein are in, fats are out.
- *Hydration.* Coaches used to say, "Don't drink before a workout or you'll get a stitch." Not anymore. Today, the best advice is drink before, during, and after a workout.
- *Fun.* Make sure that training is enjoyable. It's all about increasing your capacity for fun.

# – 6 –

# Health and Safety

This chapter focuses on several things that can go wrong in the wilderness. Chances are, they won't happen. The same type of list could be drawn up for accidents around the home, so don't worry—just be prepared.

Many of these problems are preventable or treatable with one antidote—knowledge.

## Altitude Sickness

Most of us live near the bottom of a 10-mile-deep ocean of air. This air, having weight and being compressible, becomes denser as it gets deeper.

At sea level, we are adapted to this density, or pressure, which is 15 pounds per square inch. When we gulp in air, that 15 pounds of pressure forces sufficient oxygen through the thin linings of our lungs, giving our blood what it needs to sustain us.

As one goes higher, the pressure diminishes. At 10,000 feet, it is down to 10 pounds, and much less oxygen is forced through the linings of the lungs. As a result, the blood may carry as much as 15 percent less than its normal load of oxygen, a shortfall that can cause headaches, fatigue, and shortness of breath. At 18,000 feet, the air pressure is only half what it is at sea level, and almost no one escapes unpleasant symptoms. For most, mental processes are dulled, decision making suffers, vision weakens, and the simplest exertion takes a physical toll.

DON SERL

Avoid altitude sickness by acclimatization: Do not gain more than 2000 feet per day in altitude.

The best solution is acclimatization. Move up from sea level incrementally. Not everyone will be affected by altitude sickness at the same rate, but everyone will experience some symptoms if they go high enough fast enough. Going light and fast can help you avoid bad weather and descend before high-altitude symptoms really set in, but, the more acclimatization the better. As a general rule, do not gain more than 2,000 feet per day in altitude.

There is evidence that climbers adapt a little better if they have regularly been to high altitudes, but everyone still must go through the acclimatization process no matter how many times they have been at high altitudes. Even accomplished climbers of Himalayan peaks will be off their game, perhaps severely, if they go from sea level to 12,000 feet without acclimatizing.

Here are some other things to keep in mind when climbing at high altitudes:

- Climb high, then return low to sleep.
- Avoid excessive exercise until fully acclimatized.
- Drink plenty of fluids at all times.

- If you descend, remember that your hard-won acclimatization is lost in a few days. Do not reascend rapidly to altitude.
- Beware of pills that mask the symptoms of altitude sickness, allowing you to carry on and ignore physiological deterioration.
- Conditioning seems to help a little, but the main criterion for successful adaptation to high altitude is the hypoxic drive to breathe. Simply put, this is a measure of how much compensatory breathing you do when your tissues get underoxygenated, as they do at altitude.

## Bivouacs

If you are trying to avoid a bivouac, start early. That also helps you get around problems like avalanches and afternoon thunderstorms. If you figure it will take eight hours to do the approach and climb, and the storms usually hit around 2:00 in the afternoon, you should start before 6 AM. Add a cushion of time to cover things that might go wrong, because things always do. They may be small things, causing little delay, and you may finish early. If so, go for a swim, relax, or climb another peak before you head home. Starting early and finishing early will help lessen the dangers of avalanche and afternoon thunderstorms. Thunderstorms give some warning—the message is to get down as fast as you can. Avalanches are a lot less forgiving. In all but the smallest slides you're out of control. A number of factors like fresh snow and temperature changes can make for bad avalanche conditions. Obvious precautions like avoiding cornices and not breaking trail across a leeward slope after a snow storm help, but for slide prone areas you should pick up a book on the subject.

If there's much of a chance you'll have to spend the night, carry a bivouac sack with mesh to keep out biting insects. A bivy sack, which weighs maybe a pound, can add immeasurably to your comfort level. A tent adds even more comfort, but it also adds several extra pounds to your load.

An emergency option, if conditions permit, is to build a snow cave. A snow cave provides shelter from the elements, making an ideal bivouac site for a mountaineer. Winds will not affect you, and with luck, avalanches should roll right over you as well. A snow cave is far warmer than a tent at night but pleasantly cooler in the heat of the midday sun. The disadvantages of a snow cave are that it is tiring,

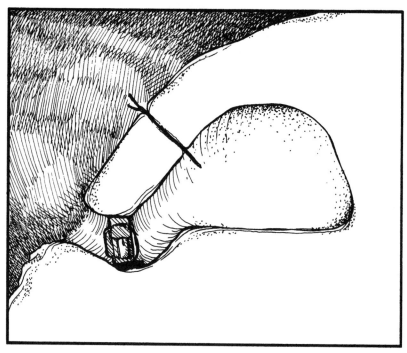

A snow cave: If the temperature is well below freezing, a snow cave can be built in a slope of firm snow at least 6 feet deep. Dig an entryway into the slope at least 3 feet deep, then hollow out a domed area large enough for you and your equipment. Use your pack to keep the entrance clear, and be sure to create an opening overhead for ventilation.

time-consuming work to dig one, and it's not always easy to find the soft, deep snow you need.

A forced bivouac with no tent, bivy sack, or snow cave is the least comfortable and potentially most dangerous option, though there is a big difference between one bivouac and a series of them. Each night will likely be damper and colder than the one before.

When choosing a bivouac site, keep in mind that the landscape is ever changing. Thus, you should avoid camping beneath loose rock or in an avalanche chute. Obvious? A friend of mine once came upon a group setting up camp at the bottom of a gully. He said to them, "You know, this is a lousy place to camp. There's a cornice right up there, and if it heats up, it could come crashing down on you."

The leader, who was a professional guide, became defensive, rejecting the advice. So my friend withdrew, going over to the other side of the cirque to climb. It wasn't long before he heard a loud roar. Sure enough, the cornice had given way and had come crashing down on the group. It was a miracle that nobody was killed. As it was, snow buried most of their packs, forcing them to abandon the climb.

Sleeping on a ledge below loose rock carries similar risks. If the loose rock is snow encrusted and gets early-morning sun, move out early in the morning before it heats up.

Here are some other tips:

- Look for shelter protected by an overhang, which will shield you from rain and rockfall.
- If you bivouac in a forest, sleep right next to a tree, which will be warmer than out in the open.
- If your perch is precarious, anchor yourself to the land.
- If sleeping in talus or loose rock, build a rock barrier to prevent rolling off.
- If traveling where others have gone before, look for sleeping areas already flattened out.

## Weather

When you climb—and especially when you bivouac—you need to be conscious of the weather. Tune in to the climatic rhythms. Pay attention to the general weather patterns. For example, it's common for afternoon thunderstorms to bully the mountains in the summer. If you're aware of that, you won't be lulled into a false sense of security by an azure-sky morning. As the day goes on, look for a buildup of cumulus clouds that could augur afternoon thunderstorms.

Become a cloud watcher. Clouds offer important clues to what weather will do. *Cirrus* clouds are the highest in the sky. They are indistinct, fuzzy clouds, composed of ice crystals, and are associated with fair weather, but only temporarily. Appearing as much as a thousand miles ahead of a front, they typically provide a few hours' to two days' warning of an approaching storm. If you see wispy cirrus clouds, keep an eye on the sky for signs of cloud buildup.

*Stratus* clouds come in waves, layers, or bands. When the waves are smooth and regular, expect fair, cool weather; when the waves become irregular or break up into a buttermilk sky, a storm is probably brewing.

*Cumulus* clouds have flat bottoms and puffy tops. Normally they indicate fair weather. If, however, they billow upward, mass together,

Changes in cloud forma-
tions will indicate
approaching storms.

DON SERL

and darken into towering, anvil-shaped *cumulonimbus* clouds, a thunderstorm is imminent.

Pay attention to the direction and intensity of winds, important
clues in the prediction of weather. Wind also plays an important role
in our physical comfort. Moving air has a chilling effect on the human
body that makes the temperature seem lower. *Windchill*, a measure of
the cooling power of both temperature and wind, is a more valid comfort indicator than temperature alone.

On a hot day, the cooling effect of air brushing against the body is
pleasant. As the temperature drops, however, windchill can be dangerous.

For example, a temperature of 5 degrees F. combined with a light
breeze of ten miles per hour equals a windchill temperature of minus
15 degrees F.

This is a potentially critical drop (and one not measured by a con-
ventional thermometer), as frostbite strikes much more quickly at
minus 15 degrees.

Pay attention to the elevation, which you can determine from

Cloud formations (*from bottom to top*): Stratus clouds come in waves, layers or bands; cumulus clouds are lumpy and billowy, with flat bottoms and puffy tops; cumulonimbus clouds are darkened, towering storm clouds; and cirrus clouds are wispy, fuzzy clouds high in the sky.

topographical maps. Elevation affects both temperature and precipitation; expect cooler, wetter weather as you climb.

Another meteorological hazard is lightning. Thunder is impressive, but it's lightning that is the real danger. It streaks across the sky at 60,000 miles per second, lasting but a few thousandths of a second, and withers anything in its path. The risk of being stuck by lightning exceeds most other outdoor risks. Every year in the United States alone, hundreds of people are killed by lightning—far more than are killed by snakes, spiders, bears, bees, or mountain lions—and three times that many are wounded. Watch the sky for cloud buildup. In the mountains, the afternoons are generally more dangerous than the mornings.

---

To estimate how far away lightning is, when you see a flash of lightning, start counting until you hear thunder. Every five seconds equals about a mile.

---

If you get caught in a lightning storm, don't handle metal objects like fishing rods, your ice ax, or tent stakes, and get rid of your metal belt buckle. If you are outside, seek shelter in a building if possible. If not, take refuge in a cave (but not near the mouth), ditch, canyon, or cluster of small trees. In a grove of trees, stay away from the tallest ones. When there is no shelter, avoid the highest object in the area, such as a lone tree. You're better off crouching in the open than remaining near an isolated tree. Also avoid hilltops, open boats or fields, wire fences, exposed sheds, and any elevated, electrically conductive objects. If you are caught in the open, crouch down, touching the ground with only your feet. Even better, stand or sit on something dry and nonconducting, such as a foam pad or sleeping bag.

If you begin to feel the electrical charge—your hair stands on end, your skin tingles, you glow in the dark—immediately drop to the ground.

When it comes to treatment, remember that a direct hit of lightning can deliver 200 to 300 million volts for up to a tenth of a second. With such a short duration, severe burns are uncommon; more likely, a victim will suffer ruptured eardrums, cardiac or respiratory arrest, or damage to the brain or spinal cord. The respiratory center in the brain may be paralyzed and breathing may stop while the heart keeps beating. Artificial respiration may be necessary. Begin CPR immediately, even if the person appears to be dead. People frequently survive direct hits of lightning.

## Loose Rock

A lot of beginners do not wish to climb loose rock. But in the high mountains, with rampant frost fracturing, you will have to climb loose rock if you intend to get anywhere. If you don't want to climb loose rock, don't go mountain climbing.

Some rock will rattle and seem precariously loose but actually fits together neatly, like a jigsaw puzzle. Other times you may be able to climb loose rock just fine, only to have your rope dislodge something. Strategically place protection to relocate your rope so that it protects all members of your team.

Quite often, loose rock will break off if you pull straight out but will be fine if you press down on it. Test it first; if the risk seems too great, go around it.

## Route Finding

It's important for mountain climbers to be good route finders. This involves more than just finding the easiest way up—it means finding the safest and easiest way up. Sometimes you must choose a more difficult but safer route, because the alternative is too dangerous.

## Ice

Ice is easier to climb when it's frozen solid, so start as early as possible, before things heat up. With an ice ax and crampons, you can make holds wherever you need them, eliminating the need for extensive searching. That convenience and the reflective properties of ice make it easier to climb ice in the dark than rock.

A good way to test ice is to throw a hefty rock at it and watch what it does. I was once considering jumping down about 6 feet onto a steep ice patch. Because the temperature was above freezing, I thought the ice would be soft enough to grab and hold me. But when I threw a rock at it, it bounced off as though the ice were metal, and I knew it would be a mistake to jump onto it, so I scrambled to its edge and cut steps with a rock. Other times, the snow has been so soft that my rock has started a snow slide. When it's that sloppy, look for a firmer route.

**Ice climbing is safest early in the day, before temperatures begin to rise.**

Don Serl

## Steep Snow

Like ice, snow is easier to negotiate when it's really cold. Depending on how much the snow has melted the previous day and how hard it has frozen at night, it can be as hard as ice in the morning—ideal for crampons—but so soft and slushy later in the day that it's hard to rig a belay anchor or use an ice ax.

Starting early reduces the chances of your creating an avalanche or of one spontaneously starting above you. Moreover, it's less tiring to climb on top of hard snow than it is to trudge through soft snow.

A few years ago, I was part of a three-man team doing a four-day traverse of the Mount Waddington range, a crest of 9 peaks, on a 13,260-foot mountain northwest of Vancouver. In the heart of a range that parallels the Pacific shores of Canada, Waddington is host to a great amount of snowfall and glaciation. Because of softening snow later in the day, we couldn't belay, so we weren't even roped up. Suddenly, a big chunk of ice broke off and started tumbling toward us. One of my partners tried to duck it, but it clipped him in the shoulder, almost knocking him over backward.   If it had, he would have

Plan to climb early or late in the day in snow and ice, when temperatures keep ice at its hardest.

DON SERL

dropped about a thousand feet. We shouldn't have been on the snow slope that late in the day. We usually climbed early, snoozed in the afternoon, then climbed again until well past midnight. After about three hours of sleep, we'd be up by five o'clock to climb while the snow was still hard. It was safer and less exhausting to do it that way.

## Wet Rock

Take care on wet rock, which can be slippery. It's a potentially greater problem if it's covered with lichen or moss or is glacial polished, with round, smooth holes rather than angled or square-cut ones.

## Falling

Sometimes falling is not extremely dangerous, and other times it is. All other things being equal, it's more dangerous to fall in the mountains than at a roadside crag. I've taken thousands of falls and haven't suffered a serious injury from any of them. Each time I was roped or close to the ground, as in, say, a boulder problem.

If you're climbing with a rope and putting in protection, the steeper the rock the better. What's critical is not how far you fall, but what you hit. Even a short fall onto a hard ledge can crack an ankle, whereas a big roped fall on a steep wall leaves you unscathed—at least physically.

If you're climbing a face and fall, there's not much you can do except to try to avoid hitting your head. If you fall while on a slab, panic will often spur you to find a way to stop. Once while climbing in Canada, I hit some slime and started skidding, then sliding. I rolled onto my side and directed my body toward the short, shallow side of the slab, avoiding the long, steep side. I was eventually able to self-arrest by grabbing a cedar branch.

---

On my first trip to Yosemite in 1979, I had my worst climbing accident. It was a fall—by someone else. I was climbing Royal Arches and, although we didn't know it, there was a party above us. I had just tied on to a ledge when I heard a jangling sound. I looked up to see a guy 25 feet above me and dropping like a stone. Fortunately for him, I stopped his fall; unfortunately for me, I did it with my face. I took a lot of stitches, had to wear a patch over my eye, and jammed my shoulder and neck so severely that I couldn't sleep on my left side for the next five years.

The next day I took a bus back to Canada. Long bus rides are tough anyway, but in this case it was miserable. I was hurting and looked hideous, with bandages all over my face.

---

## Injuries

Once I learned to run uphill and walk downhill, I have had fewer injuries. Still, few athletes escape completely unscathed, and I am no exception. One time, climbing a roof, I was in such good shape I felt like I could do anything, which probably made me careless. Reaching out with a foot, I missed rock, twisting my body awkwardly and ripping something in my shoulder. As it turned out, I had torn both the rotator cuff and connective tissue underneath. I couldn't climb for five months, and for much of that time I didn't know if I'd ever climb again. I learned not to listen to my friends, most of whom had inapplicable anecdotes about their own shoulder problems.

Sports injuries tend to be very specific, so if yours persists for more than two or three weeks, go see a specialist.

## Equipment

Always check the condition of your equipment before you leave home. If you like to live foolishly on the edge, you will simply throw your gear in a pack and check its condition once you reach the high country—when it's too late.

## Partners

Mountain tragedies have occurred that were due to partner incompatibility. I would not want to do a hard climb with someone I didn't get along with. It's important to feel tight with your partner, to be able to depend on one another. The better you know someone, the easier it is to read them for signs of trouble, like hypothermia or altitude sickness.

I've climbed so much with my friend Dave Schultz that we can do a long day of hard routes without much talk. With a stranger, it's always, "Did you get that?" and "Let's do it this way." You have to worry, which drains energy. Climbing with a friend will help you figure out whether that person is a truly good friend. The stresses of climbing can either cement or dissolve relationships. Dave and I have cemented ours through climbing.

## Food

It's not a bad idea to carry emergency rations, maybe some energy bars in your first-aid kit, separated from your daily food supply. But unless you are a diabetic, food is unlikely to be the critical issue. I have climbed for fifteen hours, summitting numerous peaks, all on as little as six whole-wheat Fig Newtons. My energy never flagged.

In fact, I've experimented with climbing on less and found that it usually works best. For a whole week, I once averaged twenty-five pitches and 800 calories per day, with my energy level remaining high. Then I tried eating loads the night before a climb and loads during the climb—and bonked! Climbing on an easy ridge, I became so shaky, I was afraid I couldn't get down. I assumed my blood sugar was low and tried to eat, but it didn't help. I finally was able to retreat, but it taught me an important lesson.

Different people have different rates of metabolism, though; run your own tests to see what works best for you.

COURTESY OF PETER CROFT

**Peter Croft and climbing partner Dave Schultz share some well-deserved post-climb refreshments.**

## Water

As I've said, lack of water has the potential to curtail your climbing much more quickly than lack of food. According to someone's Law of Threes, you will die if you go longer than:

> Three minutes without air
> Three days without water
> Three weeks without food

Water is critical any time of the year, especially when you are exercising. Mountain streams and lakes seem to offer the solution—the sweetest, cleanest-looking water you ever did see. But beneath the surface of these apparently pristine waterways lurks a human predator. Contaminated water accounts for most infectious diarrhea in the wilderness, a remarkably recent phenomenon. As recently as 1977, the Sierra Club backpacker's guide lauded drinking directly from wilderness water as one of the special pleasures of backcountry travel. No more. Today, primarily because of a protozoan called Giardia lamblia, it is a type of wilderness Russian roulette.

Giardiasis, the intestinal disease caused by Giardia, is an unpleasant, at times debilitating, disease that produces diarrhea, flatulence, and cramping. Symptoms last seven to twenty-one days, followed by periods of relief, then relapses.

Giardia is shed in feces, deposited in water, and ingested by a new host. Infection can occur from swallowing as few as six microscopic cysts. Before about 1978, water that looked good and was moving fast was considered safe. Today, according to the Centers for Disease Control in Atlanta, no surface water is guaranteed free of Giardia. It has been discovered in mountain headwaters and at Vasey's Paradise in the Grand Canyon, close to where water springs forth in utter purity from ancient aquifers deep in the limestone.

For climbers and backpackers, chemical treatment means either Halazone (chlorine) or Aqua Potable (iodine). But chlorine doesn't kill Giardia, and iodine gives the water a ghastly taste, although an additive is now available that neutralizes that.

The best solution is to carry a lightweight, portable filter, the best of which remove not only Giardia but viruses and bacteria, too.

## Getting Lost

The first and best defense against getting lost is to carry a map and check it periodically. Some areas are more difficult to find your way around in than others. The High Sierra tends to be user friendly, with fairly small streams and obvious drainages. Areas of high rainfall demand more vigilance; it's easy to get lost in a rain forest, with its dense foliage and swollen rivers. If you get on the wrong side of a big river, you can have problems.

It's always a good idea to take along something unnaturally color-ful in case you do get lost.

There are also times when a compass can come in handy. Once on a climbing trip in Canada, a friend and I were dropped off by heli-copter. Our plan was to climb several mountains, working our way to the ocean, but we soon found ourselves on a glacier in a total white-out. We couldn't see rocks, crevasses, or horizon. My friend kept us on course with map and compass. I walked ahead of him, able to see nothing, and lots of it. My friend could see only me, and he guided me by saying "left" or "right." In the end, though, we arrived exactly where we were supposed to.

Another time, Dave Schultz and I started the long approach to a climb at two in the morning. We would reach the base by hiking up a valley. Not too wide, not too tough—or so we thought.

Pretty soon, Dave and I had this conversation:

Dave: "Y'know, Peter, from this angle, Mount Watkins looks just like Half Dome."

Peter (with sinking heart): "Dave, that is Half Dome."

Dave: "That's impossible, Peter. That would mean we went in a circle."

Peter: "Dave, we went in a circle."

Dave: "No, there's no way we could've done that."

That was Dave's refrain: "There's no way we could've done that," he said over and over. But no matter how many times he said it, it didn't change the fact that we had done just that. In a fairly narrow valley, we had somehow gotten turned around and begun walking down the valley, and after three hours we were back where we started.

A mistake like that can be a good test of a partnership. Although Dave and I were shocked by our mistake, there was no rancor between us. In fact, we laughed about it; we both knew how important it is not to take such matters, or each other, too seriously. After that debacle, which would have sent some teams home, we recovered and did the climb in a fast time.

## Dehydration

Dehydration is a big problem at high altitude, where the air is thin, cold, and extremely dry. Hard work, heavy breathing, and sweating in the bright sunlight can lead to rapid dehydration. This can cause mus-cle cramps, loss of energy, and thickening of the blood, which can make you more susceptible to frostbite and possibly even to blood clots.

The solution is to drink lots of fluids. Drink often—more than you think you need—even if you don't feel thirsty. You won't feel like it on cold days, but do it anyway. A daily liquid intake of 4 quarts may not be enough to replace the moisture lost during twelve hours of climbing.

## Cold Weather

Mountains can be cold, windy places, and you need to take precautions. The higher you go, the colder it gets. The average temperature declines by 3 to 5 degrees F. for each 1,000 feet of altitude. As you ascend, the air gets thinner and usually drier, and thus absorbs less heat from the sun.

Temperature differences at various elevations can create wild mountain winds, and the windchill factor must be taken into account. For example, a temperature of 10 degrees F. combined with a modest 20-mile-per-hour wind will cool the body as rapidly as a temperature of minus 25 degrees F. with no wind. Neglecting to take windchill into account is a major cause of frostbite.

The solution is to take clothes for the top of the mountain as well as the bottom. In cold conditions, wear layers. Long synthetic underwear helps trap heat against the skin. Wearing a hat will help keep your entire body warm, as much heat is lost through the head. Keep your feet warm and dry, too. In extreme cold, put plastic bags between two layers of socks. Use your extra socks for mittens.

**Hypothermia.** Hypothermia is a debilitating ailment that occurs when the body's metabolism is unable to produce enough heat to compensate for the heat being lost. It means a lowered body core temperature, not just cold fingers and toes, and can be deadly. Symptoms include uncontrollable shivering, irrational thought, and apathy, making the victim incapable of self-help. Hypothermia is insidious because it can strike even when air temperatures are above freezing; moderate temperatures combined with rain and wind can be deadly.

Preventive measures include staying warm and dry, and snacking frequently. Food provides sugar for use by the muscles and for conversion into heat energy.

Members of a party should watch each other closely for developing signs. The time from initial symptoms to death can be as little as two hours, so treatment must be immediate. If you are alone and in threatening conditions, allow a wide margin of safety, either by putting on extra clothes or by putting up your shelter. Never ignore shivering or fatigue.

If a climber's body temperature has dropped so far that normal metabolic processes cannot reverse a continually declining temperature, additional outside warmth must be applied. Get the victim out of the elements and out of wet clothes. Build a fire. Put the victim in a sleeping bag and have a second person lie in the bag with him. The more skin contact, the more warmth.

Hot liquids can be given, but do not do so before external heat is applied, because the cold blood from the extremities can surge into the core region of the body, chilling it to the point of death.

**Frostbite.** Frostbite occurs when tissue, usually at the extremities, is frozen. It's not as common as it once was, thanks to better clothing. If you will be facing severe conditions, take along extra gloves and socks.

If superficial frostbite occurs, you can warm the affected areas by putting them against warm skin. Take care not to break the damaged skin, as that increases the chances of infection. As tissue thaws out, it is also more susceptible to infection, and antibiotics should be taken.

## Snow Blindness

A temporary but painful condition caused by excessive glare from ice and snow, snow blindness can occur even on cloudy days. Sunglasses with UV protection should be worn all day, even when off the snow and on light-colored rock. A wide-brimmed hat will also help shield you from some of the glare.

## Sunburn

At higher elevations, the thin atmosphere filters out fewer ultraviolet rays, leaving you at greater risk for sunburn. It may seem minor compared to frostbite or hypothermia, but the incidence of malignant melanoma, a deadly skin cancer, has risen by nearly 100 percent in the past ten years.

Prevent sunburn by using a good sunscreen and covering exposed skin whenever possible. Shade your face with a wide-brimmed hat, as one-third of all skin cancers occur on the nose and another 10 percent on the lips. Lawrence of Arabia style neck drapes attach to some hats to protect the ears and neck. If you are balding, use scalp screen.

Apply sunscreen at least thirty to forty-five minutes before going out to allow it to soak in. Apply it generously and often. Studies have shown that people tend to apply only about half the amount of sunscreen that the FDA uses to determine SPF (sun protection factor). Thus SPF 14 effectively becomes SPF 7. It takes at least an ounce to cover the average adult body.

To prevent the sunscreen from being washed off by sweat, use waterproof or water-resistant sunscreen. By law, products labeled water-resistant must protect at their SPF level even after forty minutes in water, and those labeled waterproof must protect after eighty minutes in water.

Don't forget the lips, which can also burn. Lip balm with SPF 15-plus sunblock is now available. Blistex 30 doesn't melt in a hot car or pocket.

## Rescue

Chances are you won't ever have to be rescued, but just in case, remember the following: If you are caught in an unclimbable crevasse without a rope, or cellular telephone, scream your head off. If you run into trouble someplace more visible, you can try spelling out a huge SOS with rocks or tree branches, or wave a brightly colored piece of clothing or your bivy sack at passing aircraft. As always, climbing with others rather than alone reduces the chances of needing a rescue party.

---

Here's a story that includes at least the threat of almost every topic in this chapter. It was 1984 and I was on an expedition aiming to climb several peaks in Nepal. We were moving camps higher and higher on Langtang Lirung, elevation about 23,700 feet. One day another climber and I, who were more acclimatized than the others, went ahead to check out route choices. We went up without sleeping bags or bivouac gear.

The weather had been good for weeks, and we expected it to continue. We were more than 3,000 feet above our last camp when we began to see clouds. It was such a novelty that we were slow to realize the danger. Next thing we knew, a violent electrical storm hit.

In our disorderly retreat, we had to rappel down an ice face, then onto a snow arête. We left our ropes behind so that we could move faster. Although we were not getting hit directly by the lightning, it was exploding above us and the charge was running down the ridge. We wanted to stay to one side or the other of the crest, but the easiest place to travel was right on top of it. Every so often, the charge would build up and my friend's eyeglasses, which had metal rims, would start to buzz. That's how we knew we were close to being hit.

The indirect hits of lightning felt like padded baseball bats hitting the back of the head. Each time, they threw us down onto the snow, and each time, we got up and kept moving, panic-stricken.

We reached a cliff that had been relatively easy to climb on the way up but now was covered in snow and impassable. We were forced to go back up into the storm to retrieve our ropes. By the time we returned, it was dark.

We set up a rappel, and it seemed as though the storm had abated. But all of a sudden, the nylon webbing started to glow. We dived into the snow to escape the charge, and at about that time we both had the same thought: "We aren't getting down tonight."

The idea of an unprotected bivouac at more than 19,000 feet, almost 4,000 feet above the highest elevation at which I'd ever slept, was scary. I had no idea of our survival potential, but with no down jackets, sleeping bags, or bivy gear, matters seemed pretty grim. I soon realized that the way to get through the night was to keep moving. I started hacking away at an ice slope with my ax, leading my friend to believe I'd flipped out. But movement was the key, and that's the way we spent the night: shifting positions, rolling boulders down the mountain (cool crashes and flying sparks), doing isometrics. For hours, I tensed the muscles in my feet, calves, thighs, hands, and face—tense and relax, tense and relax, hundreds of times. Near the equator, the nights are about as long as the days, and eleven or twelve hours is a long time to wait for the dawn.

It was a tough night for rest, but what should have been the worst part of the trip turned out to be one of the best. In the middle of the night, I realized we were going to make it. Our feet weren't going numb; we were cold but not dangerously so.

And at first light, we saw the mountains and valleys transformed by the snowfall into a fantasyland, one of the most beautiful sights I've ever seen. The encounter with the unknown had been frightening, but what we actually experienced hadn't been that bad. The sheer intensity of it placed it outside my normal range of experiences. I learned a lot about how I react to stress, which gave me strengths to fall back on later in other mountain ranges. It also taught me that in spite of a cold, sleepless night, you can have a positive experience.

# – 7 –

# Environmental Ethics

*Climbing is so straightforward. You either did it right
or you cheated like hell.*

—RICHARD GOTTLIEB

The basic rule of environmental ethics is to leave nature like you found it, maybe even a little improved. Don't leave anything behind, and take out other people's trash.

Ethics in the mountains go way beyond litter, however. Here are some other sensitive issues:

- *Fragile landscapes.* When traveling through fragile alpine landscapes, stick to the areas less likely to show degradation. Soft meadows in particular will display footprints for years; try to skirt them altogether.

- *Fires.* Fires are comforting, but you don't usually need them. And remember that damage to alpine areas takes a long time to repair. Bring foods that don't require cooking, or carry a stove.

- *Human waste management.* It's amazing how insensitive people can be, even those who appear to love nature. It's not uncommon, even in seemingly pristine areas, to slip behind a rock and find toilet paper blowing in the breeze.

  In most backcountry areas you are provided with no latrine, no hole in the ground. The location of the toilet is left to you. When disposing of human waste, keep in mind three main objectives: minimizing the chance of water pollution, minimizing the chance of any human or animal finding the waste, and maximizing the chance of rapid decomposition.

There are two recommended means of human waste disposal. In either case, pack out used toilet paper in plastic bags.

In low-use areas, where the risk of discovery is minimal, surface disposal of feces is preferable. Choose a dry, open, fairly level exposure, above the spring high-water line, in a place unlikely to be visited by others, well away from camp and waterways. Scatter feces with a stick to maximize exposure to sun and air.

In more popular areas, bury waste in catholes, digging down no more than 6 to 8 inches. At this level live the microorganisms that most effectively break down excrement.

- *Camping.* Rude and rowdy campers are annoying to other campers. Don't be a loud camper, and don't camp right next to other campers.
- *Dogs.* Have you ever noticed that dog owners all say the same thing: "My dog won't bite." Well, I've been charged by many dogs and bitten by a few. As the biters were charging me, the owners usually yelled, "He won't bite!" seconds before the dog jumped up and bit me.

  But even dogs that don't bite cause other problems. They relieve themselves on the trail, in the woods, by the lake; they chase animals; they make noise. Finding dogs in the mountains is like going to a romantic restaurant and having screaming kids at the next table.
- *Color of gear.* Some see brightly colored packs and tents as an assault on nature. Although I am put off by electric pink tents in the wild, a garish pack or clothing can be valuable. Say you drop your pack on the last leg of a mountain scramble and come back for it later. If it blends in with nature, you may have trouble finding it. If you're lucky, you will just waste some time looking for it; if you're unlucky, you won't find it at all. And if you ever get lost, you can more readily attract searchers' attention with clothing or gear that is a color not found in nature.

# Glossary

**abseil:** see *rappel*

**accessory cord:** thin rope, from 3 to 8 millimeters, often used for making slings and runners.

**acclimatization:** The gradual process of becoming physiologically accustomed to high altitude.

**active rope:** the length of rope between a moving climber and the belayer.

**acute mountain sickness (AMS):** a condition characterized by shortness of breath, fatigue, headache, nausea, and other flulike symptoms. It occurs at high altitude and is attributed to a shortage of oxygen. Most people don't experience symptoms until they reach heights well above 5,000 feet.

**aid climbing:** the technique of moving up a rock face resting on artificial holds. Slings, ropes, nuts, and other paraphernalia are used for physical support, not just for emergency protection or belay anchors. (Contrasted with *free climbing*.)

**aiders:** see *etriers*

**alpenstock:** a snow and ice tool; the forerunner of the modern ice ax.

**alpine:** the highest biological life zone.

**alpine style:** a method of climbing emphasizing speed and light weight, in which a mountain is ascended in a continuous push and climbers carry all necessary gear with them. (Contrasted with *siege style.*)

**Alps:** mountain range extending across western Europe, from the French Mediterranean coast to central Austria. The highest peak is Mont Blanc, 15,771 feet.

**alternate leads:** a method of climbing rock or ice in which two climbers lead alternate pitches of a climb.

**anchor:** the point at which a fixed rope, a rappel rope, or a belay is secured to rock, snow, or ice by any of various means.

**angle piton:** a metal wedge that is V- or U-shaped in cross section. Designed to fit in cracks from an inch wide (baby angles) to 4 inches wide (bongs). Angles are very stable because they contact the rock in three places.

**approach:** the distance a climber must hike from the car to the start of the climb. An approach may take anywhere from a few minutes to several days.

**arête:** a narrow, serrated ridge, usually separating two glacial valleys or adjacent cirques.

**arrest:** to stop a slip or fall on snow, usually by employing an ice ax as a brake.

**ascender:** a mechanical device, such as a Jumar, Gibbs, or Shunt, that works on a ratchet principle. The device will slide up a rope but will grip securely when it gets a downward pull, thus permitting climbers to move up a rope and not slide down. Ascender knots (see *prusik*) serve the same purpose.

**avalanche:** a sliding mass of snow or ice.

**avalanche cone:** the mass of material where an avalanche has fallen. Because the debris has been compacted by the force of the avalanche, the cone remains long after other signs of the avalanche have disappeared. In places where avalanches are common, a cone may become a permanent feature.

**backcountry:** a wilderness area lying far from populated areas.

**balaclava:** a soft, woolen hat that can be worn as a cap or pulled down over the ears and the face to give protection from wind and driving snow.

**bandolier:** a chest loop for carrying climbing equipment.

**base camp:** the largest and lowest supply camp on a siege-style expedition. The other higher camps are numbered consecutively. A base camp could also be used in an area where there are many lightweight alpine-style ascents.

**basin:** a circular or oval valley or surface depression, the lowest part of which is usually occupied by a lake or traversed by a river.

**belay:** to tend the climbing rope, ready to immediately put enough friction on the rope to hold the climber in case of a fall. Friction is generated by the rope passing around the belayer's body or through a belay device. Belaying is the primary safeguard in climbing, and its practice is universal. *Belay* also refers to the entire system set up to make belaying possible, including the anchor that holds the belayer in place.

**belay device:** any of numerous small metal gadgets that force a bend in the climbing rope, creating enough friction to enable a belayer to hold a fall. See also *descender* and *figure-eight descender*.

**bergschrund:** the gap or crevasse separating the upper ice of a glacier from the mountain wall behind.

**bight:** a loop of rope.

**big wall:** a steep cliff or face, vertical or nearly so, that is 1,000 feet or more from bottom to top.

**biner** (pronounced "beaner"): slang for *carabiner*.

**bivouac:** a night out without a tent.

**bivouac sack:** a lightweight, unfilled, waterproof nylon bag that can cover a sleeping bag, or a climber caught without a sleeping bag. Also called *bivy sack*.

**bivy:** slang for *bivouac*.

**body belay:** see *waist belay*.

**body rappel:** method of descending in which a climber threads an anchored climbing rope between his legs, returns it to the front of his body, then wraps it over a shoulder and holds it behind him with one hand.

**bollard:** a horn, or hump, of snow that can be used as an anchor.

**bolt:** a thin metal rod that is hammered into a predrilled hole in the rock to serve as a multidirectional anchor. Bolts, ranging in size from $1/4$ to $1/2$ inch, were originally used to protect free climbers on otherwise unprotectable routes and to piece together crack systems on longer climbs. Because they are left in place for subsequent climbers to use, bolts remain controversial.

**bolt hanger:** a metal piece that is attached to the bolt, allowing a carabiner to be clipped to the bolt.

**bombproof:** said of a hold or belay that will not fail, regardless of how much weight or force is put on it.

**bong:** the biggest piton, designed for cracks wider than a person's foot. Also called *bong-bong*.

**bucket:** a large bombproof hold.

**bulge:** a small overhang.

**buttress:** a section of a mountain or cliff standing out from the rest, often flanked on both sides by gullies or couloirs; somewhat wider than an arête.

**cagoule:** a long, pullover waterproof jacket.

**cairn:** a small pile of stones used to mark a trail, pass, summit, or some other feature.

**carabiner:** an oval or D-shaped metal snap-link about 3 inches long in the shape of a giant safety pin. Capable of holding a ton or more, carabiners are used for attaching the rope to anchors in rock or snow.

**carabiner brake:** a configuration of four to six carabiners arranged to provide rope friction for rappeling.

**cerebral edema:** maladaptive response to high altitude in which there is excess accumulation of fluid in the brain.

**chest harness:** a harness used in conjunction with a waist harness to attach a climber to the rope. Especially useful in glacier travel.

**chickenhead:** protruding knob on a rock face that can be used for a hold or protection.

**chimney:** a crack wide enough to accommodate a climber's entire body.

**chock:** a rock wedged in a crack or behind a flake, around which a runner can be threaded and then clipped to a rope for an anchor point. Before artificial chocks, British climbers used to carry pebbles to place in cracks; later they used hexagonal machine nuts found on railroad tracks. Today there are two basic types of chocks: wedges and hexes. Also called a *chockstone*.

**chock sling:** wire, rope, or webbing that attaches to a chock.

**chute:** a gully or couloir.

**cirque:** a steep-walled, bowl-shaped depression formed by erosion from a valley glacier.

**clean climbing:** means of ascension that leaves the rock unscarred and undamaged after the climbing team has passed.

**cleaning the pitch:** removing all the protection hardware placed by the leader.

**cliff:** a smooth, steep face of rock.

**clip in:** to attach oneself to the mountain by means of a carabiner snapped onto an anchor.

**coiling:** the various methods of looping and tying a rope so that it can be carried, all requiring a certain amount of skill to avoid kinking.

**col:** a saddle or pass between two peaks.

**cordillera:** a ridge or chain of mountains. Originally applied to the Andes, it now refers to the principal mountain range of a continent.

**cornice:** an overhanging lip of snow that forms on the leeward side of a ridge or summit. Cornices are often fragile and difficult to see, especially from above, and pose special dangers to climbers.

**couloir:** a gully often providing the main drainage for a rock face. Many couloirs are at least partially snow filled; they're natural channels for avalanches, and a bergschrund often guards the entrance.

**crack:** a gap or fracture in the rock, varying in width from a thin seam to a wide chimney.

**crag:** a low cliff, one or two pitches high.

**crampons:** frameworks of steel spikes that attach to boot bottoms for gripping ice and snow. They usually have twelve spikes, ten pointing downward and two pointing forward beyond the toe of the boot for very steep ground.

**crevasse:** a deep crack in the ice of a glacier, resulting from stress on the glacier as it moves over uneven ground. Crevasses range in size from narrow fissures to huge chasms and may be covered over with snow.

**crux:** the most difficult part of a pitch or climb (though some climbs have more than one crux).

**day pack:** a soft pack smaller than a backpack, favored by day hikers for carrying food, water, and other supplies.

**deadman:** any object that can be buried in the snow and used as an anchor point for attaching a rope. Deadmen can include snow flukes, ice axes, snow pickets, tent stakes, or plastic sacks filled with snow.

**dehydration:** a depletion of body fluids that can hinder the body's ability to regulate its own temperature. Chronic dehydration lowers a climber's tolerance to fatigue, reduces his ability to sweat, elevates his rectal temperature, and increases the stress on his circulatory system. In general, a loss of 2 percent or more of one's body weight by sweating affects performance; a loss of 5 to 6 percent affects health.

**descender:** a friction device used for descending ropes (rappeling). The most common is the figure-eight; others include ATCs and the carabiner brake. Also known as a *rappel device*.

**dihedral:** a high-angled inside corner where two rock planes intersect; shaped like an open book.

**direct:** the most direct way up a route or climb, usually the way water would take to fall down the rock. The direct tends to be steeper and more difficult than ordinary routes.

**direct aid:** the aid or equipment a climber puts weight on to progress up a rock.

**divide:** the high country separating two river systems or basins.

**double up:** to anchor two chocks close together for added protection.

**down and out:** the correct position of a carabiner gate when it is connected to an anchor.

**edging:** using the sides of climbing boots to stand on thin rock ledges.

**eight-thousander:** the term for a mountain higher than 8,000 meters (26,247 feet). There are fourteen eight-thousanders, all in the Himalayan or Karakoram ranges.

**escarpment:** an inland cliff formed by the erosion of the inclined strata of hard rocks.

**etrier:** a short, foldable ladder of three to five steps with a small loop at the top for attaching to an aid point. It is usually made from webbing sewn or knotted to form loops for the feet. Most aid climbers carry two or four etriers. A climber who has moved up to the top of an etrier will place another aid point, to which the next etrier will be clipped.

**expedition:** an organized party of mountaineers, with a definite objective, who set out to climb or explore in one of the remote ranges of the world.

**exposed:** said of a climber's route that is steep with a big drop below it.

**exposure:** a long drop beneath a climber's feet.

**extractor (nut tool):** a tool climbers use to remove chocks that have become stuck in cracks. Also called a *chock pick*.

**face:** a wall of rock steeper than 60 degrees.

**fall factor:** a numerical value indicating the severity of a fall. If protection holds, the most serious fall has a value of 2, and most climbing falls are between .5 and 1. Calculate the fall factor by dividing the distance of the fall by the length of rope between you and your belayer.

**figure-eight descender:** a metal rappeling device in the shape of the numeral 8. One hole is used to attach the device to a harness with a carabiner; a rope is passed through the other hole to provide friction for the descent.

**figure-eight knot:** one of the two main knots (the other is the clove hitch) used in the ropework system.

**finger crack:** a crack so thin that only a climber's fingers will fit into it.

**firn (névé):** well-consolidated snow reduced to a dense layer of granular crystals by alternate melting and freezing.

**first ascent:** the first time a route has been climbed.

**fist crack:** a crack the size of a fist.

**fist jam:** a secure but painful (for the beginner) way of finding a purchase on a rock. In a fist jam, the climber shoves his hand into a gap in the rock and makes a fist, swelling the hand for use as an anchor point.

**fixed protection:** anchors, such as bolts or pitons, that are permanently placed in the rock.

**fixed rope:** a rope that a climber has anchored and left in place after a pitch is climbed so that climbers can ascend and descend at will. Most expedition climbing uses fixed ropes to facilitate load carrying and fast retreat over dangerous terrain.

**flake:** a thin, partly detached leaf of rock. Also means to prepare a rope so that it won't tangle when you are using it.

**flaring crack:** a crack with sides that flare out.

**fluke:** a metal plate, shaped like a shovel blade, that is driven into the snow to form an anchor point. The blade has an attached wire to which a rope can be clipped. Any downward force on the wire serves to drive the blade deeper into the snow. A fluke is one type of *deadman*.

**fracture:** a break in a rock caused by intense applied pressure.

**free climbing:** climbing in which natural handholds and footholds are used. Hardware is used only for protection and not for support or progress. (Contrasted with *aid climbing*.)

**free soloing:** climbing without ropes, hardware, or a partner.

**French free:** using protection as handholds, but not using aiders.

**friction climbing:** ascending slabs using friction between shoes and rock or hands and rock, instead of distinct holds.

**Friend:** an active (spring-loaded) camming device inserted into a crack as an anchor point. Designed and marketed by Ray Jardine in 1978, the Friend was a major breakthrough because it allowed climbers to protect roofs and parallel cracks with minimal time spent making the placement.

**frostnip:** less severe form of frostbite.

**frost wedging:** the opening and widening of a crack by the repeated freezing and thawing of ice in the crack.

**gaiters:** nylon wraparound sleeves that cover ankles and shins to prevent snow from getting into boots.

**gear freak:** a climber who has lots of equipment but not much knowledge.

**gendarme:** a rock tower straddling a ridge, making progress difficult or impossible.

**glacis:** an easy-angled slab of rock between horizontal and 30 degrees. A slab is steeper, and a wall steeper yet.

**glissade:** a voluntary, controlled descent of a snow slope by sliding. It is fun but potentially dangerous. A sitting glissade is performed on the seat of the pants; in a standing glissade, the soles of the boots are used like skis.

**Gore-Tex:** a highly breathable material used for clothing and tents. Allows water vapor from the body to escape but will not allow rain to enter.

**gorge:** a deep, narrow valley with very steep sides.

**gorp:** a high-carbohydrate snack food made primarily from nuts and dried fruit; an acronym for "good ol' raisins and peanuts."

**groove:** a shallow, vertical crack.

**gully:** steep-sided rift or chasm, deep and wide enough to walk inside.

**hand traverse:** horizontal movement across a rock face in which the body is supported mainly by the hands.

**hanging belay:** a belay station on vertical rock that offers no ledge for support.

**harness:** a contraption worn around the shoulders or waist, usually made of wide tape, and offering convenient loops through which to clip a climber's rope and gear. If a climber falls while roped onto a harness, the shock load is distributed over a wide area. The climber also has a better chance of remaining in an upright position, lowering the risk of head meeting rock.

**hawser-laid rope:** rope made from three groups of filaments plaited together.

**headlamp:** a light that is mounted on a climber's helmet or headband.

**headwall:** the sheerest, often most difficult, section of a cliff or mountain, usually its uppermost.

**helmet:** a hard shell worn on the head as protection from falling rock.

**hip belay:** see *waist belay*.

**hold:** a protrusion or indentation in the rock that a climber can grasp with fingers (handhold) or stand on (foothold).

**horn:** a protruding piece of rock over which a sling can be hung for an anchor.

**hypoxia:** underoxygenation of the tissues.

**hypoxic drive to breathe:** a measurement of how much one breathes when tissues are underoxygenated. It is an important predictor of how well a climber will do at high altitude.

**ice ax:** a tool with many uses: for self-arrest in a fall; for a personal anchor; for balance; for cutting or scraping steps in hard snow. The ice ax consists of a blade (adze) and pick mounted on a wood or metal shaft (the spike).

**ice piton:** a piton designed to be hammered into ice.

**ice screw:** a threaded metal device with a pointed tip that is pounded, then screwed, into hard ice. It serves the same purpose as a piton in rock.

**impact force:** the tug a falling climber feels from the rope as it stops a fall.

**jam crack:** a gap in a rock that offers inadequate handholds but is wide enough for the climber to find purchase by inserting fingers, hand, fist, or feet.

**jamming:** wedging fingers, hand, fist, or feet into a crack to create an anchor point.

**jug:** a large, indented hold; a bucket. Also, slang for the verb to *jumar*.

**Jumar:** a trade name for a Swiss rope-gripping ascender. This device is so widely used for self-belay and for hauling on expeditions that the word is also used as a verb: "I jumared up to the ledge."

**kernmantle:** standard climbing rope in which a core (kern), constructed of one or more braided units, is protected by an outer braided sheath (mantle).

**knife blade:** a thin piton.

**knife edge:** an arête.

**knoll:** a small, rounded hill or mound.

**laybacking (liebacking):** grabbing a vertical edge, often a flake of rock, then pulling with hands, pushing with feet, and walking the feet up almost alongside the hands. It is a strenuous but useful technique for arêtes, corners with cracks, and cracks offset in walls.

**lead, or leader:** the first climber in a party of roped climbers; the head of an expedition.

**leader fall:** a fall taken by the lead climber. The leader will fall double whatever the distance is to the closest protection.

**leading through:** said of a second climber continuing to climb through a stance, thereby becoming the leader. If both climbers are of more or less equal competence, this is an efficient way to climb.

**ledge:** a level area on a cliff or mountain; may be grass, rock, or snow.

**load capacity:** the maximum load that a piece of gear can withstand.

**manteling:** a technique in which the climber moves up high enough to push down on a ledge with both hands until the body is supported on stiffened arms. The climber then replaces one hand with a high-stepping foot and moves up to stand on the ledge.

**massif:** a compact group of mountain peaks or high points, not necessarily a range or a chain.

**mixed route:** a route involving both rock climbing and ice or snow climbing.

**moraine:** a bank or ridge of loose rocky debris deposited by a moving glacier.

**mountain sickness:** a spectrum of maladaptions at high altitude, of which pulmonary edema is the most severe.

**multiday climb:** a climb so long or difficult that it requires more than one day to complete.

**multidirectional anchor:** an anchor that is secure no matter which direction a load comes from. Bolts, some fixed pitons, and some chock configurations are multidirectional anchors.

**multipitch route:** a climb consisting of more than one pitch.

**nailing:** hammering a chain of pitons into a crack.

**natural anchor:** a tree, boulder, or other natural feature that is well placed and strong enough to make a good anchor.

**natural line:** a rock climb that follows an obvious feature up the face of a cliff, such as a groove, gully, or series of cracks.

**niche:** a small recess in a rock face, usually large enough to hold a climber.

**nose:** a jutting protrusion of rock, broad and sometimes with an undercut base.

**nut:** an artificial chockstone, usually made of aluminum alloy and threaded with nylon cord. Nuts are fitted into cracks in the rock and usually can be used in place of pitons, which can scar the rock. A climber using only nuts needs no hammer, since nuts can be lifted out of their placements.

**objective dangers:** mountain hazards that are not necessarily the result of flaws in a climber's technique. They include avalanches, rockfall, and crevasses.

**off-finger crack:** a crack too wide to finger-jam but too narrow to hand-jam.

**off-hand jam:** a crack too wide to hand-jam but too narrow to fist-jam.

**off-width:** a crack too wide to fist-jam but too narrow to fit the whole body into.

**off-width protection:** chocks that are wide enough to anchor in an off-width.

**open book:** a high-angled inside rock corner; a *dihedral*.

**opposing chock:** a chock that is anchored in the opposite direction from another chock. In combination, the two chocks protect against a multidirectional load.

**overhang:** rock that exceeds 90 degrees.

**palming:** pressing the palm of the hand into the rock to create a friction hold.

**pass:** a deep depression between two mountains.

**pedestal:** a flat-topped, detached pinnacle.

**peg:** see *piton* (this is the British term).

**pendulum:** a sideways movement across a rock face by swinging on a rope suspended from above.

**pin:** see piton.

**pinnacle:** a partially detached feature, like a church steeple.

**pitch:** a section of climbing between two stances or belay points. A climbing distance that is usually the length of a 150- or 165-foot rope, it is the farthest the leader will go before allowing the second on the rope to catch up.

**piton:** a metal wedge hammered into a crack until it is secure, used as an anchor point for protection or aid. In the United States, pitons are used only when absolutely necessary, because repeated use damages rock. The first hard-steel pitons were made by John Salathé for use on the Southwest Face of Half Dome in 1946. Also known as *pin* or *peg*.

**piton hammer:** a hammer designed and carried for pounding in and extracting pitons.

**piton scar:** a groove in the rock caused by the placement and removal of a piton.

**pocket:** a shallow hole—and thus hold—in the rock.

**powder snow:** light, fluffy snow that has not thawed or refrozen.

**protection:** the anchors—such as chocks, bolts, or pitons—to which a climber connects the rope while ascending.

**protection system:** the configuration of anchors, runners, carabiners, ropes, harnesses, and belayer that combine to stop a falling climber.

**prow:** a rock feature resembling the prow of a ship, such as the Nose of El Capitan.

**prusik:** a technique for climbing a rope, originally by use of a prusik knot, now also by means of mechanical ascenders. Karl Prusik's knot uses a loop of thin rope wound around a larger-diameter rope in such a way that the knot will slide freely when unweighted but will grip tightly to the main rope when a climber's weight is applied to it.

**pulmonary edema:** abnormal accumulation of fluid in the lungs.

**put up:** to make the first ascent of a route.

**rack:** the collection of climbing gear carried by the lead climber, as arranged on a gear sling. Also, to arrange the gear on the sling.

**rappel:** to descend by sliding down a rope. Friction for controlling the descent is provided by wraps of rope around the body or by a mechanical rappel device. The rope is doubled so that it can be pulled down afterward. Also called *abseil*.

**rappel device:** see *descender*.

**rappel point:** the anchor for a rappel— that is, what the rope, or the sling holding it, is fastened to at the top.

**rating systems:** a system of terms or numbers describing the difficulty of climbs. There are seven major rating systems, including the American (Yosemite) Decimal, British, French, East German, and Australian systems.

**rib:** a prominent, slender feature, more rounded than an arête.

**rock-climbing boots:** soft boots with flat rubber soles designed to grip rock.

**roof:** an overhanging section of rock that is close to horizontal. Roofs vary in size from an eave of a few centimeters to giant cantilevers several yards wide.

**rope:** necessary in the belay system. Modern climbing rope is 150 or 165 feet of nylon kernmantle. Lead ropes range from 9.8 to 11 millimeters in diameter, double ropes 8 to 9 millimeters. According to John Forrest Gregory in *Rock Sport*, the ideal climbing rope would have all of the following qualities: low impact force, low elongation under both impact force and low load, good handling qualities, light weight, water resistance, high ratings for holding falls, resistance to cutting and abrasion, and a low price.

**roped solo climbing:** free-climbing or aid-climbing a route alone but protected by a rope. This is an advanced, complicated technique.

**roping up:** the act of a party of climbers tying themselves together with climbing ropes.

**route:** a particular way up a cliff. A cliff may have dozens of routes, each with a name and a rating.

**runner:** a short length of nylon webbing or accessory cord tied or stitched to form a loop; used for connecting anchors to the rope and for other climbing applications. Also called a *sling*.

**runout:** a section of a climb that is unprotectable.

**safety margin:** the amount of extra strength built into climbing gear. For example, a carabiner may have a strength rating of 6,000 pounds, but it rarely has to support more than 3,000 pounds. Thus it has a cushion, or safety margin, of 3,000 pounds.

**scoop:** an indentation in the rock face, not as deep as a niche.

**scramble:** an easy climb, usually without a rope. (Contrasted with *technical climbing*.)

**scree:** a long slope of loose stones on a mountainside.

**screwgate:** a carabiner that can be "locked" with a barrel on a screw thread. Less common than snaplinks, screwgates are used when there is a risk of the gate opening. Also called a locking carabiner.

**seam:** a crack far too thin for fingers but big enough to accept some small chocks or pitons.

**second:** the climber who follows the lead. Though the lead might take a substantial fall, the second usually risks only a short fall, as the belay is from above. The second usually cleans the pitch.

**self-arrest:** stopping oneself during a fall, often with the use of an ice ax.

**self-belay:** the technique of protecting oneself during a roped solo climb, often with a self-belay device.

**serac:** an ice tower or pinnacle, often unstable.

**siege style:** a method of climbing a mountain by setting up and stocking a series of camps along the route in preparation for an assault on the summit. (Contrasted with *alpine style*.)

**slab:** large, smooth rock face inclined between 30 and 60 degrees.

**sling:** see *runner*.

**smearing:** a technique of friction climbing where the sole of the boot is squashed into the depression to gain the best hold.

**snow blindness:** temporary but painful impairment of vision caused by glare off snow or ice.

**snow cave:** a hole dug in the snow or ice for the purpose of surviving a cold-weather bivouac. Sheltered from winds and most avalanches, it is far warmer than a tent.

**snow goggles:** dark glasses with both front and side protection to prevent snow blindness.

**soloing:** climbing alone, whether roped or unroped, aided or free.

**spike:** a finger of rock.

**spindrift:** powder snow whipped by the wind.

**squeeze chimney:** a chimney just wide enough to accommodate the body of a climber.

**stance:** the position of the belayer.

**stemming (bridging):** a climbing technique in which the climber pushes out to the sides with hands and/or feet, using opposing pressure against the rock. Often used in ascending chimneys and dihedrals.

**step-cutting:** cutting steps in ice or snow with an ice ax.

**step-kicking:** kicking the feet into firm snow to create steps.

**stopper:** a wedge-shaped nut.

**stuff sack:** a water-repellent or waterproof nylon bag with a drawstring, used for compact storage of sleeping bag or down jacket.

**suncups:** depressions in the snow caused by unequal melting.

**swami belt:** part of the harness; 10 to 12 feet of 1- or 2-inch webbing wrapped around the waist in such a way that it allows a climber to tie on to it with a rope.

**taking in:** removing slack in the active rope from a moving climber.

**talus:** the weathered rock fragments that accumulate at the base of a slope.

**technical climbing:** climbing that requires hardware, harnesses, ropes, and specialized climbing boots. (Contrasted with a *scramble*.)

**tension traverse:** direct-aid climbing in which a climber crosses a traverse with the aid of a tight rope from the side, using hands and feet on the rock to counterbalance the side pull of the rope.

**third-classing:** free-soloing a Class 4 or Class 5 route without protection.

**traverse:** to proceed around rather than straight over an obstacle; to climb from side to side. A traverse may be an easy walk along a ledge or a daunting passage. Protecting traverses is often difficult, because a fall will cause the climber to pendulum, ending up off route even if no injuries occur.

**Tyrolean traverse:** a rope bridge connecting two points (with a backup second rope linked to the climber who is crossing).

**UIAA:** The Union Internationale des Associations d'Alpinisme, an international climbing organization founded in 1932 that coordinates and fosters mountaineering interests around the world.

**unidirectional anchor:** an anchor that will hold securely if loaded from one direction but will pull free if loaded from any other direction.

**verglas:** a film of ice on rocks, too thin for crampons to penetrate, often caused by freezing mist.

**waist belay:** a method of taking in and paying out a belayed active rope. The belayer passes the rope around his waist; the hand on the active rope side is the directing hand, and the hand on the slack rope side is the braking hand. Also called the *hip belay* or *body belay*.

**wall:** a steep cliff or face, more than 70 degrees.

**wand:** a long, thin stake placed along the climbing route so that even in stormy conditions climbers can find their way back along the route.

**whiteout:** a condition of near-zero visibility caused by driving snow or fog merging with the white surface.

**windchill:** the cooling of the body that results from wind passing over its surface—especially dramatic if the surface is wet. It is a more useful measurement of meteorological discomfort than is temperature alone.